D0664049

Fodor's
2**5**BEST
New York

by Kate Sekules

Fodor's Travel Publications
New York • Toronto • London • Sydney • Auckland
www.fodors.com

Contents

KEY TO SYMBOLS

- 🗺 Map reference to the accompanying pull-out map
- ✉ Address
- ☎ Telephone number
- ◷ Opening/closing times

- 🍴 Restaurant or café
- Ⓜ Nearest subway (Metro) station
- 🚌 Nearest bus route
- 🚆 Nearest rail station

ENTERTAINMENT

126

Whether you're after a cultural fix or just want a place to relax with a drink after a hard day's sight-seeing, we've made the best choices for you.

EAT

138

Uncover great dining experiences, from a quick bite for lunch to top-notch evening meals.

SLEEP

150

We've brought together the best hotels in the city, whatever budget you're on.

NEED TO KNOW

160

The practical information you need to make your trip run smoothly.

PULL-OUT MAP

The pull-out map accompanying this book is a comprehensive street plan of the city. We've given grid references within the book for each sight and listing.

📷 Nearest riverboat or ferry stop
♿ Facilities for visitors with disabilities
🛈 Tourist information
❷ Other practical information

🖐 Admission charges:
    Expensive (over $10),
    Moderate ($5–$10) and
    Inexpensive (under $5)
▷ Further information

Introducing New York

"New York is an island off the coast of Europe." There's a lot of truth in this witticism, and it's no wonder this is the city most overseas visitors choose first. The qualities that weld New Yorkers to the city also mark them out as alien to heartland America.

Residents of Manhattan value directness, diversity and creativity; they live at a ridiculous pace; they work all hours (they have to, to pay the rent); they walk—fast—everywhere; they fail to keep their opinions to themselves; they have street smarts; they are capital L Liberal. Of the so-called Blue States—those dominated by Democrats—New York is the bluest of them all. The city that actually lived through the 9/11 attack that kicked off an era of paranoia and xenophobia refuses to give in to fear; New Yorkers have all the *chutzpah* they ever did.

Here, where some hip neighborhood is forever preparing to eclipse the last hot spot, change is the only constant. The crime-ridden, graffiti-scarred mean streets of the late 20th century are but a distant memory. In fact, terrorist threats notwithstanding, these days New York is the safest large city in America, according to the FBI Uniform Crime Report. In stark contrast to the gritty days, you'll see strollers (pushchairs) everywhere, because there is a mini baby-boom in progress. Real estate prices are in the realm of fiction, and a whole lot of regular folks have decamped for Brooklyn, while those who can't afford Brooklyn have gone to Queens. These days Harlem is all glamorous and beautiful; the Bronx is next. Staten Island, the fifth borough that most visitors know only for its ferry, is the final frontier.

For many, Manhattan will always be the center of the universe. It's where deals are done, stars are born, legends—and fortunes—are made. Nowhere else in America offers such diversity in fashion, food, design, theater and the arts. The stimulation is addictive, and simply being here is worth a thousand inconveniences. You can take in only so much of the big picture in one visit. So do as New Yorkers do—find a corner of the city and make it your own.

FACTS AND FIGURES

- Visitors in 2010: 48.7 million (a record)
- Dollars spent by visitors: $31 billion (2010)
- Hotel rooms by end 2009: 80,899
- Eating establishments: 23,499
- New restaurants in 2010: 157
- Licensed yellow cabs: 13,237
- Feature films shot in New York: over 250 a year

REAL ESTATE

New York has not escaped the fall in property prices that resulted from the sub-prime mortgage fiasco, credit crunch and the global economic downturn. But price tags remain hefty, and the city's real estate obsession continues. New Yorkers view their homes as not just their castles, but their portfolio, retirement plan and chief financial burden.

BROOKLYN

Once a separate city, the vast borough of Brooklyn across the East River has experienced a migration of disaffected New Yorkers that has changed its character forever. Once Brooklyn was deeply unfashionable; now it's a Manhattanite's nighttime destination for excellent restaurants, good music and great parties in those oh-so-desirable brownstones.

ONE WORLD TRADE CENTER

Formerly known as the Freedom Tower, the tower rising in the northwest corner of the World Trade Center Site (▷ 73) has been named One World Trade Center. When completed in 2013, it will be 1,776ft (541m) high—symbolic of the date of US independence—making it the tallest skyscraper in America. Observation decks are planned for the 100th and 101st floors.

Focus On Architecture

New York is constantly changing, and nowhere is this more apparent than in its architecture. Skyscrapers symbolize the city, but it has many other gems, from ornate art deco office lobbies to the classical columns, carvings and statuary of its Beaux Arts public buildings.

Skyscrapers Past

Although Chicago erected the first skyscraper in 1885, New York embraced the high-rise building style so grandly that it has become the hallmark of the city's skyline. Among the earliest still standing is the 1899 Park Row Building, topped by its distinctive Beaux Arts domes, which at 391ft (119m) held the title of "world's tallest building" for nine years. It was followed in 1902 by Daniel Burnham's triangular Flatiron Building (▷ 67); the 700ft (213m) Metropolitan Life Insurance Tower (1909), modeled after St. Mark's Campanile in Venice; and the neo-Gothic Woolworth Building (1913), at 792ft (241m) the world's tallest until1930.

In Lower Manhattan, skyscrapers grew so thick and fast that the streets of the Financial District started to turn into dark canyons. Zoning laws were passed in 1916, requiring builders to taper the upper storys with "setbacks" to allow light to reach ground level.

By 1930, the race for the top had become a battle of egos, as 40 Wall Street was trumped by the spire of the Chrysler Building (▷ 22–23), only to lose its title the following year to the Empire State Building (▷ 30–31). It remained the world's tallest building until the World Trade Center towers went up in 1972.

…and Present

From the 1950s onward, art deco elegance gave way to the glass "curtain wall" buildings of the International and Postmodern styles, which are so prominent in Midtown. The 21st

Clockwise from top left: Norman Foster's Hearst Tower; the triangular FlatIron Building; 19th-century Gramercy Park Historic District; interior of the U.S. Custom House,

century has seen the addition of such new landmarks to the city skyline as Norman Foster's Hearst Tower (2006), with its gleaming diagonal grid frame. When One World Trade Center (▷ 5) is completed in 2013 New York will once again be home to the tallest building in the United States.

Civic and Residential Architecture

But there's much more to New York architecture than these high-rise wonders. Outstanding among its civic buildings are several Beaux Arts beauties, including the U.S. Custom House (1907; ▷ 73), the New York Public Library (1911; ▷ 48) and Grand Central Terminal (1913; ▷ 36). SoHo's Cast Iron Historic District (▷ 52) is lined with elaborate Italianate facades.

Residential architecture is also fascinating in this commercial city, from the brick tenements of the Lower East Side with their zig-zagging fire escapes, to the fine brownstone town-houses with their high stoops and elaborate doorways lining the leafy streets of Greenwich Village or Brooklyn Heights, to flamboyant luxury apartment buildings like the Dakota and Ansonia overlooking Central Park on the Upper West Side.

Early Relics

Sadly, very little remains in Manhattan from the city's earliest days. Seek out the colonial-era St. Paul's Chapel (▷ 72), the Federal-style warehouses of Schermerhorn Row at South Street Seaport (▷ 54), The Row, a line of Greek Revival houses on the north side of Washington Square (▷ 73), or the delightful 19th-century houses surrounding Gramercy Park, once home to the likes of John Steinbeck (No. 38) and Joseph Pulitzer (No. 17). These survivors are rare gems in a city that is always tearing down the old to make room for the new in its never-ending reach for the stars.

one of New York's finest Beaux Arts buildings; The Row, Washington Square North; the spire of the Chrysler Building; the Woolworth Building's neo-Gothic facade

Top Tips For…

These great suggestions will help you tailor your ideal visit to New York, no matter how you choose to spend your time.

…Star Chefs
Jean Georges Vongerichten's restaurant (▷ 146) is the flagship of his ever-growing worldwide empire.
Daniel Boulud at **Café Boulud** will wow you (▷ 143). Don't forget the madeleines.
Good luck scoring a table at **Per Se** (▷ 148). Thomas Keller has been called the best chef in America. Often.
For fish, nobody matches Eric Ripert at **Le Bernardin** (▷ 142).

…Cutting Edge
Trot over to **Jeffrey New York** (▷ 122) to refresh your wardrobe, or, for vintage, **Resurrection** (▷ 124).
Get a taste of the LES at the **Parkside Lounge** (▷ 136).
Have a late supper at **The Spotted Pig** (▷ 149).
Check out the latest show at the **New Museum of Contemporary Art** (▷ 70) or go gallery hopping in **Chelsea** (▷ 66).

…Partying till Dawn
Friday and Saturday dance the night away to Latin grooves at **S.O.B.'s** (▷ 137).
Go with the groove at the late-night jazz series from 12.30am on Friday and Saturday at the **Blue Note** (▷ 132).
Ward off a hangover with a hearty breakfast or some Ukrainian soul food at **Veselka** (▷ 149), open 24 hours.

…Big and Beautiful Views
Harbor rooms at the **Ritz-Carlton Battery Park** (▷ 158) include a telescope.
Take in the lake view from Central Park's **Loeb Boathouse** (▷ 147).

Clockwise from top left: Vintage style for sale; view from the Top of the Rock at the Rockefeller Center; FAO Schwarz, a big hit with kids; head to the Blue Note for

Not everyone knows about the **Roof Garden Café and Martini Bar at the Met** (▷ 136). If you're not staying at **Beekman Tower** (▷ 154), visit the 26th-floor restaurant/bar. **Top of the Rock** (▷ 51) rivals the Empire State Building (▷ 30–31) for views.

…Bringing the Kids

Amaze them with the five-story Ferris wheel inside **Toys R Us**, Times Square (▷ 58–59). You can never go wrong with a zoo. **Bronx Zoo** (▷ 74) is vast; the one in **Central Park** (▷ 18–19) won't take all day.
Take them to **Serendipity 3** (▷ 149) for frozen hot chocolate.
Get tickets for **The New Victory Theater** (▷ 135).
FAO Schwarz is more than a toy store—it's a fantasyland for the child in all of us (▷ 121).

…Classic NYC

See the ceiling, covered in toy trucks at the clubby **'21' Club** (▷ 142).
Bergdorf's, Saks and **Bloomies** are classic department stores with different personalities (▷ 120, 124).
The stunning **Chrysler Building** (▷ 22–23) is New York's favorite skyscraper and an art deco masterpiece.
Walk across the **Brooklyn Bridge** (▷ 66).

…Sporting Pursuits

Here in baseball season (April to September) or post-season to October? **Yankee Stadium** (▷ 75) is a must. Or catch the Mets at **Shea**. **Madison Square Garden** (▷ 135) has it all: basketball (the Knicks), boxing, tennis, track and field…
There's a game of something in progress in **Central Park** (▷ 18–19) all summer long. If it's winter, you can skate at **Wollman Rink**. Shop for stylish outdoor sports gear at **Patagonia** (▷ 124).

late-night jazz; the pedestrian walkway, Brooklyn Bridge; Madison Square Garden; the New Museum of Contemporary Art; Café Boulud, bastion of fine cuisine

Timeline

Pre-1600 New York is populated by Native American groups.

1609 Henry Hudson sails up the Hudson River seeking the Northwest Passage.

1625 "Nieuw Amsterdam" is founded by the Dutch West India Company on the tip of Manhattan Island. The following year the colony's leader purchases the island from the Native Americans for $24 of trinkets.

THE FIGHT FOR INDEPENDENCE

In 1664 Wall Street's wall failed to deter the British, who invaded Manhattan Island and named it New York. Almost 100 years later, in 1763, the Treaty of Paris gave the British control over 13 American colonies. In 1770 the Sons of Liberty fought the British at the Battle of Golden Hill, and in 1776 the American Revolutionary War began and the British chose New York as their headquarters. The Declaration of Independence was read at Bowling Green in July 1776 and the Treaty of Paris ended the war in 1783.

1664 The British invade and rename the island New York.

1776 American Revolutionary War begins.

1783 War ends. Two years later New York becomes the capital of the United States.

1789 George Washington is sworn in as first US president at Federal Hall.

1790 Philadelphia becomes the US capital.

1807 Robert Fulton launches his first steamboat, creating trade routes that make many New Yorkers' fortunes.

1827 Slavery in New York is abolished.

1848 Start of the first great waves of immigrants.

1861 New York backs the Union during the Civil War.

Inauguration of George Washington on the balcony of Federal Hall in 1789

Immigrants arriving in New York Harbor, 1892

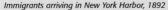

1868 The city's first "El" (elevated train) opens.

1886 The Statue of Liberty is officially unveiled.

1892 Ellis Island opens.

1904 The first subway opens.

1929 The Great Depression follows the Wall Street Crash.

1933 Prohibition ends. Fiorello LaGuardia becomes mayor.

1954 Ellis Island is closed down.

1964 Race riots erupt in Harlem and Brooklyn.

1975 A federal loan saves New York City from bankruptcy.

1990 David Dinkins, New York's first black mayor, takes office.

2001 Terrorists fly two hijacked planes into the twin towers of the World Trade Center, killing an estimated 3,000 people in the 9/11 tragedy.

2002 Rudy Giuliani's term as mayor ends. Michael Bloomberg takes office.

2011 The National September 11 Memorial opens at the World Trade Center Site, on the 10th anniversary of the attacks. A memorial museum opens in 2012.

TENEMENT LIFE

As you make your first explorations in New York, consider how it was for the early immigrants, especially those who were herded through Ellis Island, then crammed into Lower East Side tenements. Imagine how daunting the cast iron-framed SoHo buildings must have appeared to someone from, say, Vienna. Although they are now the scene of costly loft living, or home to chain stores or swank boutiques, during the immigrant boom they were sweatshop skyscrapers—symbols of hope for a fresh future. Find out more at the Lower East Side Tenement Museum (▷ 69).

Hand-outs during the Great Depression, following the Wall Street Crash of 1929

The Lower East Side Tenement Museum

⭐ **TOP 25** Top 25

This section contains the must-see Top 25 sights and experiences in New York. They are listed alphabetically, and numbered so you can locate them on the inside front cover map.

TOP 25

American Museum of Natural History

HIGHLIGHTS

- Blue whale
- Barosaurus
- Cape York meteorite
- Dinosaur halls
- Journey to the Stars
- Star of India
- Animal dioramas
- Dinosaur embryo
- IMAX theater shows

TIP

- You can observe the entire life cycle of tropical butterflies from October to June at the Butterfly Conservatory.

Of the 36 million items owned by the American Museum of Natural History—the largest such institution in the world—only a small fraction is on show. Don't miss the renowned dinosaur halls and stunning animal dioramas in native habitats.

Star attractions The original museum building opened in 1877, and as it grew its facade sported pink brownstone and granite towers, turrets and a grand Beaux Arts entrance on Central Park West. This opens into a soaring rotunda containing the museum's beloved icon: a cast of a Barosaurus rearing up to her full 55ft (17m) to protect her young from an Allosaurus attack. There's far too much to see in one day, with four city blocks and the entire evolution of life on Earth covered. In the adjoining Rose

Left: The magnificent rotunda of the American Museum of Natural History is dominated by a confrontation between an Allosaurus (left) and a Barosaurus; below: The stunning Rose Center for Earth and Space, adjoining the museum, includes the Hayden Planetarium

Center for Earth and Space, a giant sphere contains the Big Bang Theater and the Hayden Planetarium, where thrilling space shows are projected on the dome.

More gems The 563-carat Star of India sapphire is part of the Hall of Meteorites, Minerals and Gems, which contains almost $50 million worth of precious stones, plus the Cape York meteorite. Another highlight is the enormous model of a blue whale looming over the Hall of Ocean Life. The museum is best known for its splendid dinosaur halls, where real fossil specimens (rather than models) of an Apatosaurus and the first Tyrannosaurus rex ever exhibited are displayed. Equally impressive are the *tableaux morts* of animals from around the world, set in dioramas of great artistic merit.

THE BASICS

www.amnh.org

➕ C6

✉ Central Park West/79th Street

☎ 212/769-5100

🕐 Daily 10–5.45; closed major public holidays

🍴 Various

🚇 B, C 81st Street-Museum of Natural History

🚌 M7, M10, M11, M79, M86, M104

♿ Good

💰 Expensive

❓ 1-hour tours from 10.15 until 3.15. Rose Center drinks and dancing 2nd or 3rd Friday of month, 9pm–1am. Tel 212/769-5200 for advance reservations for special exhibits and events

★ 2 Brooklyn

HIGHLIGHTS

● Smith Street restaurants
● Brooklyn Heights Promenade
● Bandshell concerts
● The Theater and Rose Cinema at BAM
● Brooklyn Museum of Art

TIP

● New York Fun Tours run Best of Brooklyn Food Tasting and Multicultural Neighborhood tours three times a week (pick-up Greenwich Village; www.newyorkfuntours.com).

Brooklyn has it all—one of the largest art museums in the US and some of New York's best restaurants; beaches and a park; a zoo, aquarium and children's museum; hip neighborhoods and avant-garde arts.

Big, bigger, biggest If Brooklyn were still a separate city, it would be the fourth largest in the US. Home to more than 2 million people, it is the most populous of New York's boroughs and the most diverse, with Russian, Middle Eastern, Italian, West Indian, Hasidic Jewish and Chinese neighborhoods. The Brooklyn Museum of Art, intended by architects McKim, Mead & White to be the biggest museum in the world (it's actually the seventh largest in the US), has collections ranging from pre-Columbian art to 58 Rodin sculptures, plus what many feel are

Clockwise from far left: The Gothic arches and cables of Brooklyn Bridge; gentrified mews houses in the desirable residential area of Brooklyn Heights; Prospect Park; the excellent Brooklyn Museum of Art includes an outstanding Egyptian collection

the best Egyptian rooms outside Egypt and the British Museum. With its grand entrance, it abuts Prospect Park—opened in 1867. The Botanic Garden, zoo and the Bandshell summertime events are highlights.

The bridge and beyond A Greenway project is turning the waterfront piers into the 65-acre (26ha) Brooklyn Bridge Park, the first phase of which opened in 2010. From Brooklyn Heights you can climb stairs to the Brooklyn Bridge pedestrian crossing. Worth exploring are the brownstone neighborhoods of Park Slope, Cobble Hill and Brooklyn Heights, the latter famous for the Promenade and its view of Manhattan. Brooklyn Children's Museum has tons to do, including a miniature theater and the "Totally Tots" toddler stamping ground.

★3 Central Park

HIGHLIGHTS

- Delacorte Theater, Shakespeare in the Park
- Summer stage concerts
- Conservatory Water
- Bethesda Fountain
- Wollman Rink in winter
- Heckscher Playground
- Swedish Cottage Marionette Theatre
- Walking in the Ramble

TIPS

- Don't walk alone in isolated areas at night.
- Watch out for bicycles on the roads.

The park is the escape valve for the city. Without it New York would overheat—especially in summer, when the humidity tops 90 percent. Bikers, runners, bladers, dog strollers and frisbee players convene here. It's a way of life.

The Greensward Plan In the mid-19th century, when there was no Manhattan north of 42nd Street, *New York Evening Post* editor William Cullen Bryant campaigned until the city invested $5 million in an 840-acre (340ha) wasteland. Responsible for clearing the land was journalist Frederick Law Olmsted, who, with English architect Calvert Vaux, also won the competition to design the park, with his "Greensward Plan." Five million cubic tons of dirt were cleared to create this green space.

Clockwise from left: The Pond, at the south end of Central Park; a bronze statue inspired by characters in Lewis Carroll's Alice in Wonderland, just north of Conservatory Water; Sheep Meadow, a great place to throw frisbees; the tribute to John Lennon in Strawberry Fields

Fun and games Start at the Dairy Information Center and pick up a map and events list. These show the layout of the park and tell you about the Wildlife Conservation Center (Zoo), the Carousel, the playgrounds, rinks, fountains, statues and Strawberry Fields, where John Lennon is commemorated close to the Dakota Building where he lived and was shot. But the busy life of the park is not recorded on maps: rollerblade moves on the Mall; sunbathing in the Sheep Meadow; hanging out at the Heckscher Playground and Great Lawn softball leagues; doing the loop road by bike; sailing toy boats on Conservatory Water; birdwatching in the Ramble; jogging around the vast Reservoir; rowing on the Lake beneath the lovely Bow Bridge; fishing at Harlem Meer; or bouldering on the outcrops of Manhattan schist (rock).

THE BASICS

www.centralparknyc.org

🔲 D1–D9

☎ 212/310-6600

🛈 Dairy Information Center daily 10–5

🍴 Restaurants, kiosks

🚇 A, B, C, D, 1 59th Street-Columbus Circle; N, Q, R 57th Street-7th Avenue or 5th Avenue-59th Street, F 57th Street; 4, 5, 6 86th Street

🚌 M1, M2, M3, M4, M5, M10. Crosstown M66, M30, M72, M86

♿ Moderate

🎫 Free

HIGHLIGHTS

● Mahayana Buddhist Temple (✉ 133 Canal Street ⊙ Daily 8–7 🖪 Donation)
● Museum of Chinese in America (✉ 215 Centre Street ☎ 212/619-4785 ⊙ Thu 11–9, Fri and Mon 11–5, Sat–Sun 10–5 🖪 Moderate)
● Pearl River Mart (✉ 477 Broadway, ▷ 122)
● Doyers Street
● Columbus Park (✉ Bayard/Baxter streets)

TIP

● On a warm weekend, head for Sara Delano Roosevelt Park, near Broome and Chrystie streets, where people air their songbirds in ornate cages around the Wah-Mei Bird Garden.

New York's Chinatown has swallowed nearly all of Little Italy and has spread over a great deal of the Lower East Side. Wander here and you're humbled by the sights and sounds of a busy Asian lifestyle that thrives.

Going west Chinese people first came to New York in the late 19th century, looking to work for a while, make some money and return home. But, by 1880, some 10,000 men—mostly Cantonese railroad workers decamped from California—were stranded between Canal, Worth and Baxter streets. Tongs (bands of mafia-like operations) formed, and still keep order over some 150,000 Chinese, Taiwanese, Vietnamese, Burmese and Singaporeans. New York has two more Chinatowns: in Flushing (Queens) and Eighth Avenue, Brooklyn, with a

Clockwise from left: A colorful and vibrant area, Manhattan's Chinatown is a long-established Asian enclave and the largest Chinatown in the world; a quiet spot for a Chinese board game; a statue of Confucius; snakeskins for sale at a Chinese herbalist

further 150,000 inhabitants, but Manhattan's is the world's largest.

A closed world Although you may happily wander its colorful streets, you will never penetrate Chinatown. Many of its denizens never learn English and never leave its environs. Hundreds of factories and restaurants keep them in work; then there are the tea shops, mah-jongg parlors, herbalists and the highest bank-to-citizen ratio in New York. Catch a glimpse of this vibrant culture at the Mahayana Buddhist Temple, with its 16ft (4.8m) Buddha; in Columbus Park, where residents practice tai chi; at the fish and produce markets on Mott Street; or on tiny Doyers Street, known as "the Bloody Angle" in the early 1900s for the gang warfare that went on there.

THE BASICS

✚ F19–20

✉ Roughly delineated by Worth Street/East Broadway, the Bowery, Grand Street, Centre Street

🍽 Numerous (some close around 10pm)

🚇 J, N, Q, R, Z, 6, A, C, E, 1, Canal Street; B, D Grand Street

🚌 M22, M103

♿ Poor

❓ General tours www. explorechinatown.com Visitors' Kiosk at Canal and Baxter streets, daily 10–6

HIGHLIGHTS

● Spire
● Ceiling mural
● Elevator cabs
● Setback gargoyles
● African marble lobby

TIP

● From here Grand Central Terminal (▷ 36–37) is no distance at all. Head to the Food Court or Oyster Bar for lunch.

"Which is your favorite New York building?" goes the perennial question. Nine out of 10 people who express a preference pick the Chrysler Building. Although the public can't go beyond the lobby, it's well worth gazing upon this art deco beauty.

King for a year The tower, commissioned from William Van Alen by Walter Chrysler (who asked for something "taller than the Eiffel Tower"), won the world's tallest building competition in 1930—a title it held until the Empire State Building went up the next year. Van Alen was almost beaten by Craig Severance's Bank of Manhattan tower at 40 Wall Street, when Severance, aware of the unofficial race, slung on an extra two feet. Unknown to Severance, though, Van Alen was constructing a 123ft

Left: The Chrysler Building was inspired by a 1929 Chrysler Plymouth; middle: Visit the lobby to glimpse the building's stunning art deco interior; right: The Chrysler Building illuminated at night, viewed from the Empire State Building

(37m) stainless-steel spire, which he "slotted" through the 925ft (282m) roof, beating the 927-footer hands down. The best view of the roof of the Chrysler Building is from one of the observatories at the Empire State Building.

Multistory car Every detail of the 77-story building evokes a 1929 Chrysler Plymouth. The winged steel gargoyles are modeled on its radiator caps; the building's stepped setbacks carry stylized hubcaps and the spire resembles a radiator grill. The golden age of automobiles is further evoked by the lobby, which you can visit to see the art deco detailing in the red marble, granite and chrome interior, surmounted by the 97ft by 100ft (30m by 31m) mural depicting industrial scenes and celebrating "transportation." Don't miss the marquetry elevator doors.

THE BASICS

⊞ E11

✉ 405 Lexington Avenue/ 42nd Street

◉ Mon–Fri office hours; closed public holidays

🚇 4, 5, 6, 7, S Grand Central-42nd Street

🚌 M101, M102, M103, M42

🚆 Metro North, Grand Central

♿ Good

🎟 Free

6 Cooper-Hewitt National Design Museum

HIGHLIGHTS

- Paneling in the hall
- Solarium
- Garden
- Architectural drawings
- Summer concerts
- Textiles
- Exhibitions

TIP

- The Shop at Cooper-Hewitt is worth visiting in its own right and is open during the renovations. Many items from the changing stock are not available elsewhere.

The Cooper-Hewitt National Design Museum is closed for renovations until fall 2013. However, the shop and garden are open during this time, and exhibitions of the collection are being held at the United Nations Headquarters (▷ 72–73).

Carnegie-Hewitt The mansion that contains this superb collection belonged to industrialist Andrew Carnegie, who, in 1903, had asked architects Babb, Cook & Willard for "the most modest, plainest and most roomy house in New York City." This he did not receive (aside from the roominess), since this little chateau was built with modern conveniences galore—air conditioning and elevators—and a big gated garden to keep out the squatter neighbors. The entire neighborhood came to be

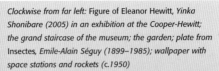

Clockwise from far left: **Figure of Eleanor Hewitt,** *Yinka Shonibare (2005) in an exhibition at the Cooper-Hewitt; the grand staircase of the museum; the garden; plate from* **Insectes,** *Emile-Alain Séguy (1899–1985); wallpaper with space stations and rockets (c.1950)*

known as Carnegie Hill. Andrew's wife, Louise, lived here until her death in 1946, then, some 20 years later, the Carnegie Corporation donated it to the Smithsonian Institution to house the Hewitt sisters' collections. The sisters, Amy, Eleanor and Sarah, had become infatuated with London's museums, and this set them collecting textiles, glass, ceramics, furniture, woodwork, metalwork and more.

And Cooper The girls' grandpa Peter Cooper (▷ 26), founder of the Cooper Union college, housed the collection here, where it stayed until 1967. Today, the Cooper-Hewitt is a vibrant place where all kinds of events happen. It also has superb reference resources, including the US's largest collection of architectural drawings and a textile library.

THE BASICS

www.cooperhewitt.org
- ✚ E4
- ✉ 2 E 91st Street
- ☎ 212/849-8400
- 🕐 Closed (except shop and garden) until fall 2013. Exhibitions during this time are being held at the United Nations Headquarters (▷ 72–73)
- 🍴 Café
- Ⓜ 4, 5, 6 86th Street
- 🚌 M1, M2, M3, M4
- ♿ Good
- 💲 Expensive
- ❓ Free tours daily

HIGHLIGHTS

● Sidewalk artists and book stalls
● Polish-Ukrainian restaurant Veselka (▷ 149)

TIP

● For a quiet break, head to Tompkins Square Park, bordered by avenues A and B, between 7th and 10th streets. Once the very definition of "needle park," it couldn't be nicer now, with fresh plantings and children playing on the lawns.

Once a haven for those priced out of Greenwich Village, East Village is now expensive bohemia. What used to be the edgiest "nabe" in town is now a youthful playground of restaurants and boutiques with a smattering of historic sights.

Early days The area was settled by Dutch, Irish, German, Jewish and Ukrainian immigrants between 1800 and 1900. By 1830, the Vanderbilt, Astor and Delano families were among those who lived in grand houses on Lafayette Street.

Notable buildings Cooper Union, founded by engineer Peter Cooper and built by 1859, is a designated landmark. It was here that Abraham Lincoln made his famous anti-slavery speech.

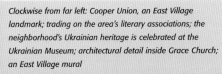

Clockwise from far left: Cooper Union, an East Village landmark; trading on the area's literary associations; the neighborhood's Ukrainian heritage is celebrated at the Ukrainian Museum; architectural detail inside Grace Church; an East Village mural

West of St. Mark's Square is the Gothic Revival Grace Church, built in 1846 by James Renwick Jr. Renwick was also responsible for the Federal-style Stuyvesant-Fish House, built in 1803 for Peter Stuyvesant, who gave it as a wedding present to his daughter and Nicholas Fish. The Ukrainian Museum is an introduction to the cultural heritage of the Ukrainians who settled here. The displays include decorated Easter eggs, ritual cloths, costumes and more.

Literary appeal A haunt of the Beat poets in the 1960s, East Village attracted Allen Ginsberg, Andy Warhol, Timothy Leary and many other radicals. Today the area has its artists and literary types, as well as budget ethnic restaurants and smart eateries offering plenty of choice for lunch.

THE BASICS

➕ F16; east of Bowery and south of 14th Street

🚇 F, M Lower East Side-2nd Avenue; 6 Astor Place

Ukrainian Museum

www.ukrainianmuseum.org

➕ F17

✉ 222 E 6th Street/2nd–3rd avenues

☎ 212/228-0110

🕐 Wed–Sun 11.30–5

♿ Moderate

★8 Ellis Island

HIGHLIGHTS

- Wall of Honor
- Treasures from Home
- Oral History Studio
- Dormitory
- Through America's Gate
- View of Lower Manhattan

TIP

- To find ancestors who landed at Ellis Island search ship passenger records in the American Family Immigration History Center on the first (ground) floor of the museum.

This museum offers a taste of how the huddled masses of new immigrants were not allowed to go free until they'd been herded through these halls, weighed, measured and rubber stamped.

Half of all America It was the poor immigrants who docked at Ellis Island after sometimes grueling voyages in steerage, since first-class passage included permission to disembark straight into Manhattan. Annie Moore, aged 15 and the first immigrant to land at Ellis Island, arrived in 1892. She was followed by some 16 million immigrants over the next 40 years, including such future success stories as Irving Berlin and Frank Capra. Half the population of the United States can trace their roots to an Ellis Island immigrant.

Clockwise from far left: Exhibition documenting the arrival of early immigrants to New York; statue of Annie Moore, the first immigrant to arrive at Ellis Island; the Great Hall; view of Ellis Island from the ferry; the view of Lower Manhattan from Ellis Island; an immigrant's records

Island of Tears The exhibition in the main building conveys the indignities, frustrations and fears of the immigrants. (As you arrive, collect your free ticket for the half-hour film, *Island of Hope/Island of Tears*, or you'll miss it.) You are guided around more or less the same route that new arrivals took: from the Baggage Room, where they had to abandon all they owned; onward to the Registry Room, now bare of furniture; and through the inspection chambers, where the medical, mental and political status of each immigrant were ascertained. The Oral History Studio brings it all to life as immigrants recount their experiences—especially moving when coupled with the poignant items in the "Treasures from Home" exhibit. This is a demanding few hours' sightseeing. Wear sensible shoes and bring lunch.

THE BASICS
www.ellisisland.org
🚹 Off map at E23
✉ Ellis Island
☎ 212/363–3200
🕐 Daily 9.30–5, extended hours in peak season; closed Dec 25
🍴 Café
🚇 4, 5 Bowling Green, 1 South Ferry, then take ferry
🚌 M5, M20, M15 South Ferry, then take the ferry
⛴ Ferry departs Battery Park South Ferry every 30 min. Ferry information, tel 877/523-9849; www.statuecruises.com
♿ Good
🎫 Museum free; ferry expensive
❓ Audio tours available

HIGHLIGHTS

- The view: by day, at dusk and by night
- The view up from 34th Street
- Observatory Audio Tour
- Marble art deco lobby

TIP

- The colored lights at the summit were introduced in 1976 and are changed to mark different events. You can avoid the line (though not the security one) by printing out advance tickets from the website.

It was not Fay Wray's fault, nor Cary Grant's in *An Affair to Remember*, that this is the most famous skyscraper in the world. Rather, its fame is the reason it has appeared in so many New York movies. You have to climb it.

King for 40 years This is the very definition of "skyscraper," and it was the highest man-made thing until the late, lamented World Trade Center was built in the 1970s. Now it is once again the tallest building in New York. Construction began in 1930, not long before the great Wall Street Crash, and by the time it was topped out in 1931—construction went at the superfast rate of four stories a week—few could afford to rent space, and they called it "the Empty State Building." Only the popularity

Left: Head to the Observatory on the 86th floor for panoramic views of New York; below: There are good views of the Empire State Building itself from 34th Street

of its observatories kept the wolves from the door. These viewpoints still attract up to four million visitors each year. The open-air 86th floor Observatory (it also has a glass-enclosed, climate-controlled area) is a highlight, but if you can't make the trip there is a virtual tour online.

The facts It is 1,454ft (443m) high, with 103 floors. The frame contains 60,000 tons of steel, 10 million bricks line the building, and there are 6,500 windows. The speediest of the 73 elevators climb about 1,000ft (330m) per minute. The fastest runners in the annual Empire State Run-Up climb the 1,860 steps (not open to the public) to the 102nd floor in just over nine minutes. The observation deck on the 102nd floor requires a separate ticket and additional fee, which is purchased on arrival.

THE BASICS

www.esbnyc.com

🚹 D13

✉ 350 5th Avenue/ W 34th Street

☎ 212/736-3100

🕐 Daily 8am–2am; last admission 1.15am

🍴 Restaurants

🚇 B, D, F, N, Q, R 34th Street-Herald Square

🚌 M1, M2, M3, M4, M5

🚉 PATH 34th Street-Avenue of the Americas

♿ Good

💲 Expensive

HIGHLIGHTS

- Shopping!
- Empire State Building
- Rockefeller Center
- The Met
- The Guggenheim
- The Cooper-Hewitt

TIP

- Try to see a parade—St. Patrick's Day Parade, the biggest, is on March 17.

Think shopping in New York and Fifth Avenue is likely to be your next thought. But there is more here: Museums, smart hotels and landmark buildings rub shoulders with FAO Schwarz, Saks Fifth Avenue and an Apple Store that never closes.

Tradition and invention Fifth Avenue runs all the way from Washington Square Park up past Central Park and houses some of the most pricey and notable real estate in New York. Walk along the avenue and you'll pass the Flatiron Building (▷ 67), the Empire State Building (▷ 30–31), the New York Public Library (▷ 48–49), Rockefeller Center (▷ 50–51), the Metropolitan Museum of Art (▷ 44–45), the Guggenheim (▷ 40–41), St. Patrick's Cathedral (▷ 71), the Frick Collection (▷ 34–35) and

Clockwise from far left: For most visitors Fifth Avenue is synonymous with shopping; Saks Fifth Avenue, one of New York's most prestigious department stores; designer brands abound; the Apple Store, a 24-hour temple of technology

the Cooper-Hewitt National Design Museum (▷ 24–25), just a few of the buildings that represent the development of Fifth Avenue.

Shop, shop, shop If you have kids, head for FAO Schwarz toy store (▷ 121). Grown-ups might prefer the jewelry emporia of Tiffany & Co. (57th Street) and Cartier (No. 653), the 24-hour Apple Store (▷ 119) or the department stores. Saks Fifth Avenue (▷ 124) has been here since 1922. Bergdorf Goodman (▷ 120) is at 58th Street, and the fashion mecca Henri Bendel is at 56th, along with the temple of stylish casual wear, Abercrombie & Fitch. If you plan to shop till you drop, two excellent hotels stand opposite each other on Fifth Avenue and 55th Street: the Peninsula New York and the St. Regis (▷ 158).

THE BASICS

➕ E16–E7
✉ From Washington Square to the Harlem River
🚇 4, 5, 6
🚌 M1, M2, M3, M4

HIGHLIGHTS

- *Mall in St. James's Park*, Gainsborough (1783)
- *Sir Thomas More*, Holbein (1527)
- *Officer and the Laughing Girl*, Vermeer (c.1657)
- *The Polish Rider*, Rembrandt (c.1655)
- *Virgin and Child with Saints*, Van Eyck (c.1441–43)
- *Philip IV of Spain*, Velázquez (1644)

Henry Clay Frick's magnificent Beaux Arts mansion on Fifth Avenue is half the reason for coming here. Henry bequeathed its riches to the nation as a memorial to himself—that's the kind of guy he was.

The man and the mansion Henry Clay Frick (1849–1919) was chairman of the Carnegie Steel Corp. (US Steel). He was a ruthless strikebreaker and one of the nastiest industrialists of his day. Instead of receiving any comeuppance (though there were assassination attempts), he got to commission Carrère and Hastings to build him one of the last great Beaux Arts mansions on Fifth Avenue and filled it with an exquisite collection of 14th- to 19th-century paintings, porcelain, furniture and bronzes. You can rest in a Louis XVI chair before strolling

Left: The oak-paneled Living Hall in the center of the mansion displays works by Holbein, El Greco, Titian and Bellini; below: The Fifth Avenue Garden

through the central glass-roofed courtyard and the gorgeous garden.

What Frick bought Some of the 40 rooms are arranged around a particular work or artist, notably the Boucher Room, east of the entrance, and the Fragonard Room, with the Progress of Love series. There are British masters (Constable, Gainsborough, Whistler, Turner), Dutch (Vermeer, Rembrandt, Van Eyck, Hals), Italian (Titian, Bellini, Veronese) and Spanish (El Greco, Goya, Velázquez). Interspersed with the paintings are Limoges enamel and Chinese porcelain, Persian carpets and Marie Antoinette's furniture.

Some Frick descendants still have keys to this modest pied-à-terre, which includes a bowling alley in the basement.

THE BASICS

www.frick.org
🚇 E7
✉ 1 E 70th Street
☎ 212/288–0700
🕐 Tue–Sat 10–6, Sun 11–5; closed public holidays
🚇 6 68th Street-Hunter College
🚌 M1, M2, M3, M4
♿ Good
💲 Expensive
ℹ Audio tours; for concerts, lectures and docent talks see calendar

HIGHLIGHTS

- Main concourse ceiling
- Oyster Bar
- Chandeliers
- Whispering Gallery
- The clock
- The 75ft (23m) arched windows
- Grand Staircase
- The Food Court (▷ 145)
- The Campbell Apartment cocktail bar

Don't call it a station. All tracks terminate here, which makes it—yes—a terminal. The Beaux Arts building bustles like nowhere else. As the saying goes—stand here long enough and the entire world passes by.

Heart of the nation "Grand Central Station!" bellowed (erroneously) the 1937 opening of the eponymous NBC radio drama; "Beneath the glitter and swank of Park Avenue… Crossroads of a million private lives!…Heart of the nation's greatest city…" And so it is, and has been since 1871 when the first, undersize version was opened by Commodore Cornelius Vanderbilt, who had bought up all the city's rail-roads, like on a giant Monopoly board. See him in bronze below Jules-Alexis Coutan's allegorical

Clockwise from far left: The concourse of Grand Central Terminal; statuary by Jules-Alexis Coutan on the main facade; Grand Central subway station; the Campbell Apartment cocktail bar; the four-faced clock; enjoy a platter of oysters in the famous Oyster Bar

THE BASICS

www.grandcentralterminal.com

➕ E11

✉ E 42nd Street/Park Avenue

☎ 212/532-4900

🕐 Daily 5.30am–2am; Story Booth daily 24 hours

🍴 Restaurant, café/bar, snack bars

🚇 4, 5, 6, 7, S Grand Central-42nd Street

🚌 M1, M2, M3, M4, M42, M101, M102, M103 Grand Central

🚆 Metro North, Grand Central

♿ Good

🆓 Free

❓ Tours Wed 12.30pm. Meet by information booth in main concourse, tel 212/935-3960. A self-guided walking tour starts at the four-faced clock

statuary on the main facade (south, 42nd Street). The current building dates from 1913 and is another Beaux Arts glory, its design modeled partly on the Paris Opéra by architects Warren and Wetmore.

Look within Inside, the main concourse soars 12 stories high, with gleaming gold chandeliers and grand marble staircases at either end. Be careful what you say here—the acoustics are amazing. Look up at the ceiling for the stunning sight of 2,500 "stars" in a cerulean sky, with zodiac signs by French artist Paul Helleu. The fame of the four-faced clock atop the information booth is out of proportion to its size. Below ground is a warren of 32 miles (52km) of tracks, tunnels and chambers; in one the famed Oyster Bar resides.

HIGHLIGHTS

● Cafés and jazz clubs
● Washington Square Park
● NYC's narrowest house (75 Bedford Street)
● Christopher Park
● Halloween Parade
● Jefferson Market Library
● Citarella and Jefferson Market (food stores)
● Minetta Lane

TIP

● Bleecker Street, one of the main drags through the Village, is lined with one-of-a-kind stores, music bars and great pizza parlors.

The Village has long been a bohemian mecca, and its picturesque neighborhoods lined with trees and brownstones form a romantic image of Manhattan.

Artists, writers, musicians Named after Greenwich in southeast London, the Village became a refuge in the 18th and early 19th centuries for wealthy New Yorkers escaping epidemics in the city. When the elite moved on, the bohemian invasion began. Edgar Allan Poe moved to 85 West Third Street in 1845. Fellow literary habitués included Mark Twain, O. Henry, Walt Whitman, F. Scott Fitzgerald and Eugene O'Neill. After World War II, artists Jackson Pollock, Mark Rothko and Willem de Kooning also lived here. Bob Dylan made his name in Village music clubs in the 1960s, while the Blue

Clockwise from far left: Bleecker Street, one of the main drags through the Village; Cherry Lane Theatre on Commerce Street is the oldest Off-Broadway theater in New York; desirable Village homes; detail of the Gay Liberation Monument in Christopher Park

Note (▷ 132) and Village Vanguard clubs remain hotbeds of jazz today.

Freedom parades When police raided the Stonewall Inn on June 28, 1969, and arrested gay men for illegally buying drinks, they set off the Stonewall Riots—the birth of the Gay Rights movement. The Inn is on Christopher Street, which became the center of New York's gay community. Statues of gay and lesbian couples stand in tiny Christopher Park. The Washington Memorial Arch (▷ 73) towers over Washington Square Park, a lively hangout for students from the surrounding New York University. As you explore, look out for the ornate Jefferson Market Library (6th Avenue and W 10th Street), the quaint Cherry Lane Theatre on Commerce Street, and tiny Minetta Lane.

THE BASICS
➕ C17
✉ East–west from Broadway to Hudson Street; north–south from 14th Street to Houston Street
🍴 Numerous
Ⓜ A, B, C, D, E, F 4th Street-Washington Square; 1 Christopher Street-Sheridan Square
🚌 M5
🚉 PATH Christopher Street
♿ Poor

HIGHLIGHTS

● The building
● *L'Hermitage à Pontoise*, Pissarro (1867)
● *Paris Through the Window*, Chagall (1913)
● *Woman Ironing*, Picasso (1904)
● *Nude*, Modigliani (1917)
● Kandinskys
● Klees
● Légers
● The store

TIP

● Museum admission is pay-what-you-wish on Saturdays 5.45–7.45, but get there early as lines can be long.

If you just happened upon Frank Lloyd Wright's space-age rotunda, your eyes would pop out of their sockets, but it's even more impressive when you follow its six-story spiral path to view the art inside.

Museum of architecture This is the great architect's only New York building. It was commissioned by Solomon R. Guggenheim at the urging of his friend and taste tutor Baroness Hilla Rebay von Ehrenwiesen, though the wealthy metal-mining magnate died 10 years before it was completed in 1959. The giant white nautilus is certainly arresting, but it's the interior that unleashes the most superlatives. Take the elevator to the top level and snake your way down the museum's spiral ramp to see why. You can study the exhibits, look over

Clockwise from left: The spiral walkway inside the Guggenheim Museum; Édouard Manet's Before the Mirror *(1876), Thannhauser Collection; the Guggenheim's curvy exterior; Vincent van Gogh's* Landscape with Snow *(1888), Thannhauser Collection*

the parapet to the lobby below and finish up where you began.

Museum of art There are some 6,000 pieces in the Guggenheim Foundation's possession. Solomon and his wife Irene Rothschild abandoned collecting old masters, when Hilla Rebay introduced them to Léger, Kandinsky, Chagall, Mondrian, Moholy-Nagy and Gleizes, and they got hooked on the moderns. See early Picassos in the small rotunda and the tower extension. For Impressionists and Postimpressionists, look for the Thannhauser Collection, always on display—unlike the rotated Guggenheim holdings, which are often shown in themed exhibitions. The museum continues to acquire works, including Agathe Snow's *Goldfinch* (2008), fashioned from debris found on local streets.

THE BASICS

www.guggenheim.org

➕ E4–5

✉ 1071 5th Avenue/89th Street

☎ 212/423-3500

🕐 Sun–Wed, Fri 10–5.45, Sat 10–7.45; closed Dec 25

🍴 Café

🚇 4, 5, 6 86th Street

🚌 M1, M2, M3, M4

♿ Good

💲 Expensive

❓ Lecture program; audio tours

HIGHLIGHTS

- Chandeliers in the Met foyer and auditorium
- Reflecting Pool with Henry Moore's *Reclining Figure* (1965)
- Lincoln Center Out-of-Doors Festival in summer
- NY City Ballet's *Nutcracker* in December
- Chagall murals in the foyer of the Met
- Free Thursday evening concerts at the David Rubenstein Atrium
- New York Film Festival
- The Revson Fountain in the Central Plaza
- Jazz at Lincoln Center
- Annual *Messiah* singalong

TIP

- Dance under the stars at the Midsummer Night's Swing in Josie Robertson Plaza, a summertime series of live band sessions.

Strolling across the Central Plaza to the fantastically lit 10-story colonnade of the Metropolitan Opera House on a deep winter's night is one of the most glamorous things you can do in this city, and you don't need tickets to come and look.

West Side Story The Rockefeller-funded über-arts center was envisaged in the late 1950s and finished in 1969, after 7,000 families and 800 businesses had been pushed aside by developer Robert Moses and the John D. Rockefeller millions. Much of *West Side Story* was filmed here after the demolition began.

All the arts The 16 acres (6ha) include mega-houses for the large-scale arts, all designed by different architects in the same white travertine.

Clockwise from left: The Revson Fountain, between the David H. Koch Theater (left) and the Metropolitan Opera House (right); the David Rubenstein Atrium is a great place to meet up with friends; Alice Tully Hall, one of several classical music venues; visitors to the Lincoln Center

The Metropolitan Opera House is the glamor queen, with her vast Marc Chagall murals, red carpet, sweeping staircase and chandeliers that thrillingly rise to the gold-leaf ceiling before performances. You can take a fascinating backstage tour. Avery Fisher Hall is home to America's oldest orchestra, the NY Philharmonic, while the Juilliard School of Music supplies it with fresh talent. The David H. Koch Theater, housing the New York City Opera and the New York City Ballet, faces Avery Fisher across the Plaza. The Franklin P. Rose Hall is the centerpiece of Jazz at Lincoln Center in the Time Warner Center. Two smaller theaters, the Vivian Beaumont and Mitzi E. Newhouse, and a more intimate concert hall, Alice Tully, plus the Walter Reade movie theater and the little Bruno Walter Auditorium, complete the pack.

THE BASICS

www.lincolncenter.org

➕ B8

✉ 70 Lincoln Center Plaza

☎ Met 212/362-6000, Avery Fisher Hall 212/875-5030, Jazz 212/258-9800

🕐 Inquire for performance times

🍴 Restaurants, cafés, bars

🚇 1 66th Street-Lincoln Center

🚌 M5, M7, M10, M11, M104, crosstown M66

♿ Good

🎟 Admission to Center free

❓ Tours leave from David Rubenstein Atrium, daily 10–4, tel 212/875-5350

HIGHLIGHTS

- Temple of Dendur (15BC)
- Period rooms, American Wing
- 19th- and early 20th-century art galleries
- *Young Woman with a Water Jug*, Vermeer (c.1662)
- *Reading at a Table*, Picasso (1934)

TIP

- Consider visiting on Friday or Saturday evening, when a string quartet serenades visitors and there are far fewer crowds.

It will give you bigger blisters than the Uffizi, bigger chills than the Sistine Chapel and take a bigger slice of vacation time than all your dining out. It's so big that it doesn't just contain Egyptian artifacts but an entire Egyptian building.

Art city The Met's limestone Beaux Arts facade with its tremendous steps was a 1902 addition to the Calvert Vaux (of Central Park fame) red-brick Gothic building buried inside. There are several more buildings-within-buildings, interior gardens and courtyards, such is the scale of the Met. The 15BC Temple of Dendur, in its glass-walled moated chamber east of the main entrance, is the best known, but there's much more besides: the Astor Court above it—a replica Ming dynasty scholar's courtyard—plus, in

Clockwise from left: The Met's European Sculpture Court; Wheat Field with Cypresses, Vincent van Gogh (1889), the European Paintings and Sculpture Room; the Beaux Arts facade of the museum

the American Wing, a score of period-style rooms, and the vast and sunlit garden court with its hodgepodge of Tiffany glass and topiary, a Frank Lloyd Wright window and the entire Federal-style facade of the United States Bank transplanted here from Wall Street.

Where to start? How to stop? A quarter of the three million-plus objects are up at any one time, so pace yourself. There are about 23 distinct collections. Some visitors decide on one or two per visit—Egyptian art, for example, or 19th- and early 20th-century European paint-ings, which include one of the largest Impressionist collections outside Paris. Others structure a route around one or two favorite works. Free guided tours of museum highlights take place daily; ask at the information desk.

THE BASICS

www.metmuseum.org

🚌 D5

✉ 1000 5th Avenue/82nd Street

☎ 212/535-7710

🕐 Tue–Thu, Sun 9.30–5.30, Fri–Sat 9.30–9

🍴 Cafeteria, restaurant, bar

🚇 4, 5, 6 86th Street

🚍 M1, M2, M3, M4

♿ Good

💲 Expensive

❓ The Cloisters (▷ 74) houses more of the Met's medieval collections; same-day admission on Met ticket

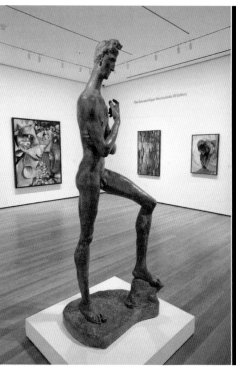

The stunning MoMA building, designed by Japanese architect Yoshio Taniguchi, has in itself been called a work of art. It opened in 2004, and has nearly twice the capacity of the old museum.

Postimpressionists to graffiti artists Founded on the 1931 bequest of Lillie P. Bliss, which comprised 235 works of art, MoMA's collections now amount to about 150,000 pieces. These include household objects, photography, graphic design, conceptual art, industrial design and media. The collection starts in the late 19th century, with the Postimpressionists and Fauvists. Among the 20th-century movements represented in the museum are Cubism, Futurism, Expressionism, Surrealism, Abstract Expressionism, Pop (Oldenburg, Dine,

Left: Gallery with Wilhelm Lehmbruck's *Standing Youth* to the fore and paintings by Chagall (left of the statue) and František Kupka (to the right); below: The stunning glass exterior of the MoMa, designed by the renowned Japanese architect Yoshio Taniguchi

Rauschenberg and Warhol) and the "Graffiti" work of Keith Haring and Jean-Michel Basquiat.

Even more modern A sunlit 110ft (33m) high atrium affords a view of the Abby Aldrich Rockefeller Sculpture Garden, a museum favorite containing such works as Picasso's *She-Goat* (1950) and Barnett Newman's *Broken Obelisk* (1963–69). Taniguchi's building features much use of glass, granite, aluminum and floods of light, and individual galleries have been designed specifically for the media they house, including contemporary art and new media. Changing exhibitions are staged on the top floor. There's a WiFi network throughout the museum, allowing visitors to download audio tours in several languages onto smart phones and other devices with HTML browsers.

THE BASICS

www.moma.org

🚼 D10

✉ 11 W 53rd Street/ 5th–6th avenues

☎ 212/708-9400

🕐 Sat–Mon, Wed–Thu 10.30–5.30, Fri 10.30–8 (Jul–Aug Thu until 8.45)

🍴 Restaurant

🚇 E, M 5th Avenue-53rd Street; B, D, F 47th–50th streets-Rockefeller Center

🚌 M1, 2, 3, 4, 5, 7

♿ Good

💲 Expensive; free Fri 4–8

HIGHLIGHTS

● Patience and Fortitude
● Main Reading Room
● Jefferson's handwritten
Declaration of
Independence
● Astor Hall
● American Jewish Oral
History Collection
● Gottesman Hall ceiling

TIP

● It's worth taking one of
the free one-hour tours of
the library (Mon–Sat 11, 2,
Sun 2). Meet at the recep-
tion desk in Astor Hall.

Why are we sending you to a library on your vacation? Because the New York Public Library's Central Research Building is a great, white, hushed palace, beautiful to behold even if you have no time to open any of its books.

The building Carrère and Hastings (who also designed the Frick, ▷ 34) were the architects of what is generally thought to be the city's best representative of the Beaux Arts style—the sumptuous yet classical French school that flourished from 1880 to 1920 in New York. In 2011 the library was discreetly rechristened the Stephen A. Schwarzman Building, after the Wall Street financier who donated $100 million towards its renovation. A pair of lions, which Mayor LaGuardia named Patience and

Clockwise from far left: The Main Reading Room of the New York Public Library; Astor Hall, the starting point of guided tours; the exterior of the library, one of the finest Beaux Arts buildings in New York

Fortitude, flank the stair that leads into the white marble temple of Astor Hall. Inside, see temporary exhibitions in the Gottesman Hall, and look up! The carved oak ceiling is sublime. Priceless items from the library's collection, such as the first Gutenberg Bible brought to the New World, line the balcony corridor or are displayed in upstairs rooms. Don't miss the stunning two-block-long reading rooms, or the Richard Haas murals of NYC publishing houses in the De Witt Wallace Periodical Room.

The books The library owns more than 18 million books, most kept in the 82 branches. This building is dedicated to research. The CATNYP computer can disgorge any of the 16 million manuscripts or three million books from the 92 miles (148km) of stacks in 10 minutes flat.

THE BASICS

www.nypl.org
+ D11–12
⊠ 476 5th Avenue/42nd Street
☎ 212/930-0800
🕐 Mon, Thu–Sat 10–6; Tue–Wed 10–8, Sun 1–5; closed public holidays
🍴 Kiosks outside (summer)
🚇 4, 5, 6, S Grand Central-42nd Street, 7 5th Avenue
🚌 M1, M2, M3, M4, M5, M7, M42
🚆 Metro North, Grand Central
♿ Good
🎫 Free

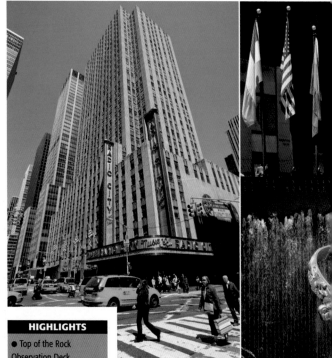

HIGHLIGHTS

● Top of the Rock Observation Deck
● GE Building's lobbies and the Lee Lawrie friezes
● NBC Studio tour
● Skating in winter
● Radio City Music Hall
● *Prometheus* (1934)
● *Atlas* (5th Avenue, 50th–51st streets)

TIP

● Pick up a free *Rockefeller Center Visitor's Guide and Walking Tour* at the information desk in the GE Building. It points out the center's artworks and the stories behind them.

This complex of art deco buildings provides many of those "Gee, this is New York" moments, especially at Christmas when you see ice-skaters ringed by the flags of the UN and gaze up at the massive tree.

Prometheus **is here** The 19-building Rockefeller Center has been called the greatest urban complex of the 20th century. John D. Rockefeller Jr.'s grand real estate scheme provided work for a quarter of a million people during the Depression. Its centerpiece is the elongated ziggurat GE Building (formerly the RCA building) at 30 Rockefeller Plaza, adorned with Lee Lawrie's glass-and-limestone frieze, lobby murals by José Maria Sert and various other artworks. Rest for a while on a Channel Gardens bench and gaze on the Lower Plaza,

Left: Radio City Music Hall forms part of the Rockefeller Center; middle: Paul Manship's Prometheus *(1934) on the Lower Plaza; right:* Friendship Between America and France *(1934), a gilded bronze by Alfred Janniot above the Fifth Avenue entrance*

the ice rink and Paul Manship's gilded bronze *Prometheus* (1934).

Top of the Rock The three-tiered observation deck at the top of the GE building affords stunning panoramic views over Manhattan and the only such public view over Central Park. The mezzanine museum tells the history of the complex before high-speed elevators whisk you to the 67th–70th floor viewing platforms.

NBC and Rockettes The GE Building also houses NBC Studios. Take a studio tour or join the line for standby tickets for *Saturday Night Live*. Over on Avenue of the Americas is the Radio City Music Hall, home to NBC and the Rockettes, who star in the annual Christmas Spectacular, one of the top shows in town.

THE BASICS

www.rockefellercenter.com

✚ D10

✉ 5th–6th avenues/ 48th–51st streets

☎ 212/632-3975

🕐 Various

🍴 Many restaurants, cafés

Ⓔ B, D, F, M 47th–50th streets-Rockefeller Center

🚌 M1, M2, M3, M4, M5, M7, M50

♿ Moderate

🎟 Free

❓ Radio City tours, tel 212/247-4777; NBC Studio tours, tel 212/664-3700; Rockefeller Center tours, tel 212/698-2000

Top of the Rock

www.topoftherocknyc.com

☎ 212/698-2000

🕐 Daily 8am–midnight (last shuttle 11pm)

💲 Expensive

HIGHLIGHTS

- King and Queen of Greene Street
- Little Singer Building
- Haughwout Building
- Gallery browsing
- Shopping

TIP

- Stop at Dean & DeLuca (Broadway and Prince) for a coffee and pastry, a hot sandwich, or to browse its delectable gourmet fare, including its cheese and dessert counters.

Once known for its artists' lofts and cutting-edge galleries, SoHo has moved upmarket. Its cobbled streets and cast-iron buildings now teem with designer boutiques, trendy shops, and pricey bars and restaurants.

Cast in iron An acronym for "South of Houston", SoHo stretches for several delightful blocks between Houston and Canal streets, bordered by Lafayette Street on the east and Sixth Avenue to the west. Around 500 of its 19th-century industrial buildings have been pre-served in the SoHo Cast Iron Historic District. Cast-iron architecture was not only strong and fire-resistant, but enabled ornate buildings in Italianate and other elaborate styles to be erected quickly and cheaply. Some of the finest examples are the King (Nos. 72–76) and

Clockwise from far left: The Little Singer Building in the SoHo Cast Iron Historic District; sculpture inspired by the well-known 1932 photograph of New York ironworkers eating lunch while sitting on a girder; one of many fashionable stores; a great place to stroll; art galleries abound

Queen (Nos. 28–30) of Greene Street, the Little Singer Building (561 Broadway) and the Haughwout Building (488 Broadway), which had the first Otis steam elevator. Old-fashioned lampposts and block paving stones further enhance SoHo's charm.

Art and fashion By the 1960s and '70s, many of SoHo's commercial buildings were abandoned. Artists moved in, art galleries followed, and SoHo became the hippest quarter in town. Rising prices forced many artists and galleries to Chelsea and beyond, but fashionistas quickly filled the spacious showrooms. Everything from Prada's flagship store to branches of Bloomingdale's and London's Topshop to designer boutiques such as Nicole Miller and Vivienne Tam make this a shopper's heaven.

THE BASICS

- E18–19
- Houston–Canal streets, Lafayette Street–6th Avenue
- Numerous
- N, R Prince Street; 6, C, E Spring Street
- M5, M21
- Good

21 South Street Seaport

- View of Brooklyn Heights
- Richard Haas's Brooklyn Bridge mural
- The historic buildings of Schermerhorn Row
- Harbor cruise on the *Pioneer*
- Titanic Memorial Lighthouse
- Fulton Market (especially the bakeries)

TIP

- For information on summer concerts, fireworks and other events, visit www.southstreetseaport.com.

This reconstructed historic maritime district, with its cobbled streets, is a tourist trap. However, when you stroll the boardwalk on a summer's night, with the moon over the East River, you are very glad to be a tourist.

Pier, cruise, shop, eat The seaside/cruise-ship atmosphere is what's fun at the Pier 17 Pavilion, which juts 400ft (122m) into the East River, overlooking Brooklyn Heights. It's a mall, with chain stores, bad restaurants and a food court, but it also has three stories of charming wooden decks, where you can watch the boats plying the river beneath the Brooklyn Bridge (▷ 66). Check out Richard Haas's *trompe-l'oeil* mural of the bridge on the north side of Peck Slip, between Front and South streets. The adjoining piers, 16 and 15, house several

Clockwise from far left: The Peking, the second-biggest sailing ship ever built; the renovated Federal-style warehouses of Schermerhorn Row; view of Brooklyn Bridge from South Street Seaport; cobbled Fulton Market, which has good cafés and bakeries

historic vessels, including the 1885 schooner *Pioneer* and the 1930 tugboat *W. O. Decker*, both of which give harbor cruises between May and September. The 1812 Federal-style warehouses of Schermerhorn Row—Manhattan's oldest block of commercial buildings—contain galleries, shops and restaurants, and there are cafés in Fulton Market.

Many museums The Seaport Museum Visitor Center acts as a clearing house for the exhibitions here. One ticket admits you to the second-biggest sailing ship ever built, the *Peking*; the lightship *Ambrose*; the Children's Center; the Seaport Museum Gallery; a recreation of a 19th-century printer's shop; and walking tours (including "Ship Restoration" and "Back Streets"—worthwhile if you have time).

THE BASICS

www.seany.org

🔲 F21

ℹ️ Visitor Center,
12 Fulton Street. Tickets
also from Pier 16

☎ 212/748–8725

🕐 Most shops Mon–Sat
10–9, Sun 11–8; Museum
Apr–Dec Tue–Sun 10–6;
Jan–Mar Thu–Sun 10–5,
ships 12–4; Schermerhorn
Row galleries only Mon
10–5. Closed Dec 25 and
Jan 1

🍴 Numerous

🚇 2, 3, 4, 5, J, M, Z Fulton
Street; A, C Broadway-
Nassau Street

🚌 M15 Pearl/Fulton Street

♿ Poor

💰 Expensive

HIGHLIGHTS

● View from the crown
● Statue of Liberty Museum
● Fort Wood, the star-shape pedestal base
● Her centenary flame

TIP

● Visits to the crown must be reserved in advance on tel 201/604-2800 or online at www.statuecruises.com. There are no same-day crown tickets.

The green lady, symbol of the American dream of freedom, takes your breath away, however many times you've seen her photograph—and despite her surprisingly modest stature.

How she grew In the late 1860s, sculptor Frédéric-Auguste Bartholdi dreamed of placing a monument to freedom in a prominent location. His dream merged with the French historian Edouard-René de Laboulaye's idea of presenting the American people with a statue that celebrated freedom and the two nations' friendship. Part of the idea was to shame the repressive French government, but, apparently, New Yorkers took their freedom for granted: It was only after Joseph Pulitzer promised to print the name of every donor in his newspaper, the

Left: Liberty Island, a beacon of hope since 1886; middle: Liberty's seven-pointed crown; right: The symbol of American liberty raises her torch to the world

New York World, that citizens coughed up the funds to build the pedestal. Liberty was unveiled by President Grover Cleveland on October 28, 1886.

Mother of exiles Emma Lazarus's stirring poem *The New Colossus* is engraved on the pedestal, while the tablet reads: July IV MDCCLXXVI—the date of the Declaration of Independence. Beneath her size 107 feet, she tramples the shackles of tyranny, and her seven-pointed crown beams liberty to the seven continents and the seven seas. Gustave Eiffel designed the 1,700-bar iron and steel structure that supports her. She weighs 225 tons, is 151ft (46m) tall, has an 8ft (2m) index finger and a skin of 300 copper plates. The torch tip towers 305ft (93m) above sea level.

THE BASICS

www.nps.gov/stli
- Off map at E23
- ✉ Liberty Island
- ☎ 212/363-3200
- 🕐 Daily 9.30–5; extended hours in peak season. A limited number of daily tickets to tour the pedestal/museum may be reserved in advance from ferry office, by phone or online
- 🍴 Cafeteria
- 🚇 4, 5 Bowling Green, 1 South Ferry, then take ferry
- 🚌 M5, M15, M20 South Ferry, then take ferry
- 🚢 Departs Battery Park South Ferry (AF19)
- ☎ 877/523-9849; www.statuecruises.com
- ♿ Poor
- 💲 Free; ferry expensive

HIGHLIGHTS

● New Victory Theater
● Shubert Alley
● Indoor Ferris wheel at Toys R Us
● ABC's *Good Morning* studio: 44th/Broadway
● New Year's Eve ball drop

TIP

● The TKTS booth, located at Duffy Square, 47th Street/Broadway, sells same-day theater tickets for 20–50 percent off. The booth is open daily 3–8 for evening shows (from 2pm Tue); Wed and Sat 10–2 for matinees; Sun 11–8 for all shows.

"The Crossroads of the World," one-time symbol of Manhattan glitz and glam, is an area New Yorkers love to hate—especially since it has been sanitized. You may disagree as you explore the big stores and get dazzled by the neon.

The Longacre The junction of Broadway and Seventh Avenue was called "The Longacre" until Times Tower, the new home of the *New York Times*, was finished in 1904. Almost immediately, the invention of neon light, the opening of the first subway and the decision to site the New Year celebration here conspired to make it the de facto center of Manhattan.

On Broadway The theaters moved in to the area and Broadway, the Great White Way,

Clockwise from far left: Detail on the old Paramount Theater, a Times Square landmark; New Victory Theater, which specializes in family entertainment; bright lights, big city; the indoor Ferris wheel at Toys R Us; visitors flock to Times Square for shopping, family attractions and the full-on neon

became synonymous with bigtime showbiz: its popular theatrical—especially musical—division. By 1914 there were 43 theaters in the immediate vicinity of the square; after multiple closings, refurbishments and re-openings, there are 22 of them today.

Best of Times, worst of Times By the 1970s Times Square was one of the most crime-ridden neighborhoods in the city, rife with drug-dealing and porn emporia of all kinds. But a massive clean-up effort in the 1990s brought about its rebirth. Today it's a tourist hotspot, with family attractions, megastores and restaurants beneath the glittering state-of-the-art illuminations. Parts of Times Square are now car-free, though the human traffic jams are bigger than ever.

THE BASICS

www.timessquarenyc.org

⊞ C11

🛈 Times Square Visitor Center, 1560 Broadway/ 7th Avenue

☎ 212/768-1560

🕐 Mon–Fri 9–8, Sat–Sun 8–8

🚇 1, 2, 3, 7, N, Q, R, S Times Square-42nd Street

🚌 M5, M7, M20, M42, M104

❓ Free "Times Square Exposé" tour, Friday at noon

HIGHLIGHTS

- Trinity Church
- Federal Hall
- New York Stock Exchange
- Mosaic lobby at 1 Wall Street

TIP

- Stand on the top step of Federal Hall to get the famous photo of the New York Stock Exchange, shot over the shoulder of the statue of George Washington.

Depending on your point of view, Wall Street is the boon or bane of the world's economic fortunes. But either way, the historic buildings and urban buzz of this financial powerhouse are fascinating to see and experience.

The Buttonwood Agreement Wall Street, named for the Dutch colonial wall that once marked the city's northern boundary, is the epicenter of the financial district. It has been so since the late 18th century, when businessmen gathered here under a buttonwood tree to trade bonds, issued to raise funds for the Revolutionary War. In 1792, 24 traders signed the Buttonwood Agreement, which formalized their dealings and created the New York Stock Exchange. Today the NYSE is the largest stock

Clockwise from far left: The New York Stock Exchange; the soaring towers of Wall Street; Federal Hall, fronted by a bronze statue of George Washington and modeled on the Greek Parthenon; the beautifully decorated domed ceiling in the entrance of Federal Hall

THE BASICS

www.nyse.com
www.nps.gov
www.moaf.org
www.trinitywallstreet.org

➕ E22

✉ NYSE, 18 Broad Street; Federal Hall, 26 Wall Street; Museum of American Finance, 48 Wall Street; Trinity Church, Broadway at Wall Street

☎ Federal Hall 212/825-6990; Museum of American Finance 212/908-4110; Trinity Church 212/602-0800

🕐 Federal Hall Mon–Fri 9–5; Museum of American Finance Tue–Sat 10–4; Trinity Church Mon–Fri 7–6, Sat 8–4, Sun 7–4

🍴 Restaurants, pubs

🚇 2, 3, 4, 5 Wall Street; J, Z Broad Street

🚌 M5

🎟 Federal Hall free; Museum of American Finance inexpensive; Trinity Church free

❓ Tours: www.thewall streetexperience.com

exchange in the world. The 1903 building, with its grand trading floor and facade of Corinthian columns, stands at the corner with Broad Street. It is no longer open to the public.

A million-dollar stroll At the west end of Wall Street stands Trinity Church (1846), the third on this site. The original, built in 1699, was the city's first church. Alexander Hamilton and other famous New Yorkers are buried in the church-yard. The art deco skyscraper at 1 Wall Street houses the Bank of New York, the city's oldest. George Washington was sworn in as America's first president at Federal Hall, modeled on the Parthenon and now a national memorial and museum. Forty Wall Street is owned by Donald Trump. At No. 48, the Museum of American Finance has displays on financial history.

25 Whitney Museum of American Art

More modern than the Modern, the Whitney wants to be as unpredictable as the *artiste du jour* and often succeeds. It's a New York tradition to sneer at the Biennial, whether or not you have seen the show.

No room at the Met Sculptor and patron of her contemporaries' work, Gertrude Vanderbilt Whitney offered her collection to the Met in 1929, but the great institution turned up its nose and Whitney was forced to found the Whitney. In 1966, Marcel Breuer's cantilevered, granite-clad Brutalist block was completed to house it in a suitably controversial manner—a building that is not universally loved but impossible to overlook. The Whitney's collection now reads like a roll call of American 20th-century greats: Edward Hopper, Thomas Hart Benton,

Left: Dempsey and Firpo *by George Bellows (1924), a highlight of the Whitney's collection; below: The cantilevered granite-clad building designed by Marcel Breuer was a controversial addition to Madison Avenue*

Willem de Kooning, Georgia O'Keeffe, Claes Oldenburg, Jasper Johns, George Bellows and Jackson Pollock are a few. Let's hope the curators and buyers are as good as Gertrude at spotting talent.

Take your pick Exhibitions, drawn from the museum's important and delicious collection, often emphasize a single artist's work. At other times they prove more eclectic. There's an active film and video department, and plans are underway for a new building in the Meatpacking District. The Whitney Biennial (in the spring of even-numbered years) presents the curator's vision—often controversial—of the leading trends in American art during the past two years and often features the work of young or lesser-known artists.

THE BASICS

www.whitney.org
+ E7
⊠ 945 Madison Avenue/ 75th Street
☎ 212/570-3600
🕐 Wed–Thu, Sat–Sun 11–6, Fri 1–9; closed Thanksgiving, Dec 25, Jan 1
🍴 Café
Ⓜ 6 77th Street
🚍 M1, M2, M3, M4
♿ Good
💰 Expensive
❓ Exhibitions, events; free daily tours

More to See

This section contains other great places to visit if you have more time. Some are in the heart of the city while others are a short journey away, found under Further Afield.

In the Heart of the City

AMERICAN FOLK ART MUSEUM
www.folkartmuseum.org

The outstanding collection of quilts is a highlight in this museum spanning the rich variety of folk art, from paintings and pottery to textiles and woodcarving, and dating from the 18th century to the present day. The museum's shop stocks a superb range of handcrafted items.

🚊 C8 ✉ 2 Lincoln Square ☎ 212/595-9533 ⏰ Tue–Sat 12–7.30, Sun 12–6 🚇 1 66th Street-Lincoln Center 💲 Free

BATTERY PARK
www.thebattery.org

At the southernmost tip of Manhattan, with splendid views of New York Harbor, Battery Park was named for the cannon sited here to defend the fledgling city against British attack. Ferries to the Statue of Liberty and Ellis Island leave from Castle Clinton National Monument, a former fort. Among the monuments in the park, look for *The Sphere*, which once stood at the World Trade Center plaza and serves as a memorial to 9/11.

🚊 E23 ✉ Tip of Manhattan 🚇 1 South Ferry; 4, 5 Bowling Green

BROOKLYN BRIDGE
Completed in 1883, the Brooklyn Bridge was the first to link Manhattan and Brooklyn. With its twin Gothic towers and graceful ballet of cables, it is one of New York's finest landmarks. Stroll across the pedestrian walkway for views of the Manhattan skyline.

🚊 G21 🚇 4, 5, 6 Brooklyn Bridge-City Hall; A, C High Street/Brooklyn Bridge

CHELSEA
North of Greenwich Village is the neighborhood of Chelsea. Its landmark Chelsea Hotel (222 W 23rd Street), made famous in Andy Warhol's film *Chelsea Girls*, was home to a roll-call of artists, musicians and writers including Thomas Wolfe, Dylan Thomas, Arthur Miller and Arthur C. Clarke, who wrote *2001: A Space Odyssey* here. It is filled with works by resident artists, who often donated art in lieu of rent. The Chelsea Art District, from

The American Folk Art Museum

Chelsea Hotel, a favorite haunt of artists, writers and musicians

19th to 29th streets between 10th and 11th avenues, has eclipsed SoHo with its concentration of galleries. Also here are Chelsea Art Museum (556 W 22nd Street), with exhibitions of contemporary art, Chelsea Market (▷ 121), the Chelsea Piers sports complex on the Hudson River (enter on 23rd Street), the High Line (▷ 68) and the Rubin Museum of Art (▷ 71).

🔲 A–D13–15 ✉ From 30th Street south to 14th Street, and 6th Avenue west to the Hudson River 🚇 1, 14th, 18th, 23rd, 28th streets-7th Avenue; C, E 14th, 23rd streets-8th Avenue

CITY HALL

www.nyc.gov
Built between 1803 and 1812 in Federal and French Renaissance styles, this is one of the nation's oldest city halls. The building and the rotunda, with its Corinthian columns and coffered dome, are designated landmarks. See the Governor's Room furniture and portrait collection on a guided tour.

🔲 E20 ✉ Broadway/Murray Street ☎ 311 or 212/639-9675 🕐 Thu 10am, advance reservation required 🚇 2, 3 Park Place; 4, 5, 6 Brooklyn Bridge-City Hall; R City Hall 🎟 Free

ELDRIDGE STREET SYNAGOGUE

www.eldridgestreet.org
Built in 1887, this synagogue is a symbol of the aspirations of Eastern European immigrants on the Lower East Side. Its 50ft (15m) vaulted ceiling, Moorish and Romanesque details, and stained-glass windows make it an architectural gem. Exhibits and free guided tours point out design features and tell the story of this diverse neighborhood.

🔲 G19 ✉ 12 Eldridge Street ☎ 212/219-0302 🕐 Sun–Thu 10–5, Fri 10–3 🚇 F East Broadway; B, D Grand Street 🎟 Moderate

FLATIRON BUILDING

This 1902 skyscraper designed by Daniel Burnham was named for its amazing and memorable shape: an isosceles triangle with a sharp angle pointing uptown.

🔲 E14 ✉ 175 5th Avenue/E 22nd–23rd streets 🚇 N, R 23rd Street

Eldridge Street Synagogue on the Lower East Side

GRACE CHURCH

www.gracechurchnyc.org

This James Renwick-designed Gothic Revival church dating from the mid-19th century has superb stained glass and a mosaic floor.

⊞ E16 ✉ 802 Broadway ☎ 212/254-2000 ⏰ Mon–Fri 10–4, Sun services 🚇 N, R 8th Street-NYU; 6 Astor Place ❓ Free guided tours Sun 1pm

HIGH LINE

www.thehighline.org

An elevated freight railroad above 10th and 11th avenues, abandoned in 1980, has been turned into a park and promenade. The first phase of the High Line runs from Gansevoort Street in the Meatpacking District to W 20th Street, with plans to extend it to 34th Street. There are benches, sun loungers, artworks and views over the Hudson waterfront. Elevators make it accessible to wheelchairs and strollers.

⊞ B16–B15 ✉ Access at Gansevoort Street, 14th, 16th, 18th and 20th streets ☎ 202/500-6035 ⏰ Daily 7am–10pm 🚇 1, 2, 3, A, C, E 14th Street 🎫 Free

INTERNATIONAL CENTER OF PHOTOGRAPHY

www.icp.org

The ICP's permanent collection has 60,000 images from the 1930s to the present. They include photographs by Henri Cartier-Bresson, Elliott Erwitt and Harold Edgerton, along with 13,000 original prints by Weegee, who photographed crime scenes and New York nightlife in the 1930s and 1940s.

⊞ D11 ✉ 1133 Avenue of the Americas/43rd Street ☎ 212/857-0000 ⏰ Tue–Thu 10–6, Fri 10–8, Sat–Sun 10–6 🚇 B, D, F, M 42nd Street-Bryant Park 🎫 Expensive

ITALIAN AMERICAN MUSEUM

www.italianamericanmuseum.org

In the heart of Little Italy, this small museum explores the history of the quarter and the rich heritage of its Italian immigrants. Exhibits range from New York policeman Frank Serpico's guns to a collection of marionettes from the 1920s and 1930s.

⊞ F19 ✉ 155 Mulberry Street/Grand Street ☎ 212/965-9000 ⏰ Wed–Thu, Fri 11–8, Sat–Sun 11–6 🚇 J, Z Canal

The Italian American Museum documents the rich history of Little Italy

Street-Centre Street; N, Q, R, 6 Canal Street-Broadway 🚇 Donation (moderate)

JEWISH MUSEUM
www.thejewishmuseum.org
The largest Jewish museum in the Western hemisphere chronicles Jewish experience worldwide. Artifacts in the permanent collection cover 4,000 years of Jewish history, while special exhibitions focus on Jewish culture, art, famous figures and more.
➕ E4 ✉ 1109 5th Avenue/92nd Street
☎ 212/423-3200 🕐 Sat–Tue 11–5.45, Thu 11–8, Fri (Mar–Oct) 11–5.45 🍴 Café
🚇 4, 5, 6 86th Street 🎟 Expensive; free Sat

LOWER EAST SIDE TENEMENT MUSEUM
www.tenement.org
This reconstruction of life in an 1863 tenement block is a must for history buffs. Different tours focus on the homes and workshops of Jewish, Italian and Irish immigrants, and there are also walking tours of the neighborhood. Tours leave from the museum shop.
➕ G18 ✉ 108 Orchard Street

☎ 212/982-8420 🕐 Tours daily 10–5
🚇 F, J, M, Z Delancey Street-Essex Street; B, D Grand Street 🎟 Expensive

MEATPACKING DISTRICT
www.meatpacking-district.com
Bordered roughly by Jane and W 14th streets west of Greenwich Street/Ninth Avenue, this district of cobbled streets was named for its wholesale meat warehouses. It is now filled with hot nightclubs and late-night restaurants. Come after dark to see what all the fuss is about, unless you want to shop in its designer boutiques, from Stella McCartney to Moschino.
➕ C16 🚇 A, C, E 14th Street

MORGAN LIBRARY & MUSEUM
www.themorgan.org
This collection of literary works, rare musical manuscripts and artworks is one of the finest in the world. Started by financier John Pierpont Morgan at the end of the 19th century, its highlights include the ninth-century Lindau Gospels, a vellum copy of the Gutenberg Bible, scores by Beethoven, Mozart

New York's Jewish Museum chronicles the history of Jews worldwide

The sumptuous Morgan Library & Museum

and Puccini and manuscripts by Jane Austen, Charles Dickens and Mark Twain.

🔸 E12 ✉ 225 Madison Avenue/E 36th Street ☎ 212/685-0008 🕐 Tue–Thu 10.30–5, Fri 10.30–9, Sat 10–6, Sun 11–6 🚇 6 33rd Street; 4, 5, 6 7 Grand Central 💷 Expensive

EL MUSEO DEL BARRIO

www.elmuseo.org

This museum dedicated to Latin American and Caribbean art contains over 8,000 items from pre-Columbian artifacts to modern paintings and photographs. There is also a program of events.

🔸 E2 ✉ 1230 5th Avenue/104th Street ☎ 212/831-7272 🕐 Tue, Thu–Sat 11–6, Wed 11–9, Sun 1–5 🚇 6 103rd Street 💷 Donation (moderate)

MUSEUM OF THE CITY OF NEW YORK

www.mcny.org

Rotating exhibitions illustrate the changing life of the city since 1624. It has an outstanding collection of photographs, as well as toys, furniture and decorative arts.

Special walking tours are available.

🔸 E2 ✉ 1220 5th Avenue/103rd Street ☎ 212/534-1672 🕐 Tue–Sun 10–5 🚇 6 103rd Street 💷 Moderate

NEUE GALERIE NEW YORK

www.neuegalerie.org

Dedicated to early-20th-century German and Austrian art and design, this marvelous gallery includes Gustav Klimt's portrait known as "Golden Adele".

🔸 E5 ✉ 1048 5th Avenue/86th Street ☎ 212/628-6200 🕐 Thu–Mon 11–6 🍴 Café 🚇 4, 5, 6 86th Street 💷 Expensive

NEW MUSEUM OF CONTEMPORARY ART

www.newmuseum.org

The dynamic building resembling giant white boxes stacked askew is a fitting home for this cutting-edge museum of contemporary art. The seventh-floor balcony affords panoramic views of Lower Manhattan.

🔸 F18 ✉ 235 Bowery/Prince Street ☎ 212/219-1222 🕐 Wed–Sun 11–6, Thu 11–9 🍴 Café 🚇 N, R Prince Street 💷 Expensive

Neue Galerie New York

The dynamic New Museum of Contemporary art

NEW YORK CITY POLICE MUSEUM

www.nycpolicemuseum.org

Visit a prison cell, learn about forensics and see a wealth of cops and robbers material including handguns, uniforms and shields. The NYPD Hall of Heroes has a memorial to the heroes who died on 9/11.

➕ F22 ✉ 100 Old Slip ☎ 212/480-3100 🕐 Mon–Sat 10–5, Sun 12–5 🚇 2, 3 Wall Street 👋 Moderate

PALEY CENTER FOR MEDIA

www.paleycenter.org

The museum's archive of 100,000 LTV programs and commercials spans nearly 100 years. When you arrive, make a reservation to use the computer catalog on the fourth floor to locate what interests you, then reserve it and watch it on one of the consoles. Or you can take in a show or two in one of the screening rooms or theaters.

➕ D10 ✉ 25 W 52nd Street ☎ 212/621-6800 🕐 Wed–Sun 12–6, Thu 12–8, Fri theater programs 🚇 E, M 5th Avenue-53rd Street 👋 Moderate

RUBIN MUSEUM OF ART

www.rmanyc.org

The superb collection of art from Tibet and the Himalayan region is the largest in the West. Religious art and cultural artifacts include scroll paintings, sculptures, ritual objects, textiles, masks and prints.

➕ D15 ✉ 150 W 17th Street/Seventh Avenue ☎ 212/620-5000 🕐 Mon, Thu 11–5, Wed 11–7, Fri 11–10, Sat–Sun 11–6 🍴 Café 🚇 1 18th Street-7th Avenue 👋 Moderate

ST. PATRICK'S CATHEDRAL

www.saintpatrickscathedral.org

With its ornate spires soaring 330ft (100m) above Fifth Avenue, James Renwick's Gothic Revival cathedral, built in 1858–79, seats 2,200 people. The St. Michael and St. Louis altar was designed by Tiffany & Co, while the rose window is one of stained-glass artist Charles Connick's finest creations.

➕ E10 ✉ 5th Avenue between E 50th and E 51st streets ☎ 212/753-2261 🕐 Daily 6.30am–8.45pm; services at various times; tours on request 🚇 6 51st Street; E, M 5th Avenue-53rd Street 👋 Free

Archive images, New York City Police Museum

Revisit old commercials and TV and radio programs at the Paley Center for Media

ST. PATRICK'S OLD CATHEDRAL

www.oldcathedral.org

New York's first Roman Catholic cathedral opened in 1815, when the area was settled by Irish immigrants. The present building, from 1868, has a stunning hand-carved altarpiece filled with statuary.

E18 263 Mulberry Street/Mott and Prince streets 212/226-8075 (call for times) Daily 8–5 but hours may vary N, R, Q Prince Street Free

ST. PAUL'S CHAPEL

www.trinitywallstreet.org

Opened in 1766, this is the only remaining Colonial-era church in Manhattan. George Washington worshiped here after his inauguration. St. Paul's escaped destruction on 9/11 and became a round-the-clock refuge for rescue workers. In the churchyard is the Bell of Hope, a gift from the City of London on the first anniversary of the tragedy.

E21 209 Broadway at Fulton Street 212/233-4164 Mon–Fri 10–6, Sat 10–4, Sun 7–3 2, 3, 4, 5, A, C, J, Z Fulton Street Free

TRUMP TOWER

Ride the escalators to admire the 1980s glitz. The six-story atrium has shops, greenery and waterfalls, while the top floors include "The Donald's" penthouse and the boardroom from the US version of *The Apprentice* television show.

E9 721 5th Avenue/56th Street 212/832-2000 Daily 8am–10pm Several E, M, N, R 5th Avenue

UNION SQUARE

Named for the union of Broadway and Fourth Avenue, this is where downtown and uptown meet. It is ringed with shops and restaurants and four days a week has the city's best greenmarket (▷ 125).

E15 E 14th–17th streets, Park Avenue South, Broadway Greenmarket Mon, Wed, Fri, Sat 8–6 Numerous 4, 5, 6, L, N, Q, R 14th Street-Union Square M3 Poor

UNITED NATIONS HEADQUARTERS

www.un.org

Take a guided tour to see the General Assembly Hall and art and

The flags of member nations flying high at the United Nations Headquarters

artifacts donated from around the world. Exhibitions of the Cooper-Hewitt National Design Museum are being held here during renovations of the museum (▷ 24–25).

🚇 G11 ✉ 1st Avenue/46th Street ☎ 212/963-4475 🕐 Daily 9–5.30 (visitor entrance closes 4.45) 🍴 Café, restaurant 🚇 4, 5, 6, 7 to Grand Central 💲 Expensive

U.S. CUSTOM HOUSE

www.americanindian.si.edu
Also known as the Alexander Hamilton U.S. Custom House, this 1907 Beaux Arts beauty, designed by Cass Gilbert, now houses the Smithsonian's National Museum of the American Indian, highlighting native cultures of North, Central and South America.

🚇 E22 ✉ 1 Bowling Green ☎ 212/514-3700 🕐 Museum Fri–Wed 10–5, Thu 10–8 🚇 4, 5 Bowling Green; 1 South Ferry 💲 Free

WASHINGTON SQUARE

www.washingtonsquarenyc.org
The square is a prime people-watching spot in Greenwich Village. At the north end,

Washington Memorial Arch, designed by Stanford White, marks the start of Fifth Avenue. Notice "The Row" of Greek Revival homes (Nos. 1–13, 19–26) where the elite of 19th-century New York lived—read Henry James's *Washington Square*.

🚇 D17 🚇 N, R 8th Street-NYU; A, B, C, D, E, F, M 4th Street-Washington Square

WORLD TRADE CENTER SITE

www.national911memorial.org
The National September 11 Memorial, on the site of the Twin Towers, comprises two square waterfalls cascading 30ft (9m) into pools that disappear into a center void. The pools are surrounded by bronze panels with the names of those who died, and a memorial park with more than 300 oak trees. A museum is due to open in 2012, and well underway are a new transportation hub by Santiago Calatrava and the tower at One World Trade Center (▷ 5).

🚇 D21 ✉ Church to West streets, Vesey to Liberty streets ☎ 212/267-2047 🚇 E World Trade Center 💲 Free

The splendid Beaux Arts architecture of the U.S. Custom House

Washington Memorial Arch, Washington Square

Further Afield

BRONX ZOO

www.bronxzoo.com

The biggest city zoo in the US has over 4,000 animals and is a leader in wildlife conservation. Don't miss the Congo Gorilla Forest, or the Wild Asia Complex with its monorail riding high above tigers, rhinos and elephants.

➕ Off map to northeast ✉ Fordham Road (Bronx River Parkway Northeast) ☎ 718/367-1010 🕐 Apr–Oct daily 10–5; Nov–Mar 10–4.30 🍴 Restaurant 🚇 2, 5 West Farms Square-East Tremont Avenue 💷 Expensive

THE CLOISTERS

www.metmuseum.org

A 12th-century Spanish apse attached to a Romanesque cloister and a Gothic chapel—what's all this doing in the Bronx? This is the Met's medieval branch. The bulk of the art and architecture, which is arranged chronologically, was amassed by sculptor George Gray Bernard in the early 20th century. Much was rescued from ruin: The effigy of the Crusader Jean d'Alluye, for instance, was doing duty as a bridge, while the priceless Unicorn Tapestries were acting as frost blankets.

➕ Off map to north ✉ Fort Tryon Park, North Manhattan ☎ 212/923-3700 🕐 Mar–Oct Tue–Sun 9.30–5.15; Nov–Feb Tue–Sun 9.30–4.45; closed public holidays 🚇 A 190th Street 💷 Expensive

CONEY ISLAND

www.coneyisland.com

At the end of the 19th century, Coney Island on a peak day played host to a million people. By 1921 a boardwalk and the subway had arrived. Since then, attractions have come and gone, but the big-dipper ride, the Cyclone, is still there and Nathan's Famous hot dogs are still sold from the original site. A newer attraction is KeySpan Park, home of the Brooklyn Cyclones baseball team. Look out for concerts held here in summer. Also on Coney Island is the New York Aquarium, with thousands of sea creatures from sea horses to beluga whales. A new Luna Park, named after the earlier amusement park, opened in 2010, bringing Coney Island into

Bronx Zoo, the largest city zoo in the US

One of the Unicorn Tapestries, a highlight of the Cloisters, the medieval branch of the Met

the 21st century with a range of modern thrill rides.

➕ Off map to south ✉ Surf Avenue, Boardwalk; Aquarium: W 8th Street, Surf Avenue ☎ Sideshow 718/372-5159; KeySpan Park 718/449-8497; Aquarium 718/265-3474; Luna Park 718/373-5862 🕐 Aquarium daily 10–5, summer weekends and holidays 10–7 🍴 Cafeteria at Aquarium 🚇 D, F, N, Q Coney Island-Stillwell Avenue 🎫 Aquarium, Luna Park, expensive

QUEENS

The major attractions here are the New York Hall of Science and Queens Museum of Art, both at Flushing Meadows-Corona Park. The former is a hands-on science and technology museum with a great Science Playground for children (111th Street; tel 718/699-0005). The Queens Museum of Art (New York Building; tel 718/592-9700; www.queensmuseum.org) holds exhibitions of art, Tiffany glassware and a scale panorama of New York. Outside stands the Unisphere—the world's largest globe.

➕ Off map to east

STATEN ISLAND

There are several historic sights here. Alice Austen House (2 Hylan Boulevard, tel 718/816-4506; www.aliceausten.org) is a museum of photographs by Alice Austen in her Victorian home. Historic Richmond Town (441 Clarke Avenue, tel 718/351-1611; www.historicrichmondtown.org) recreates life in a 19th-century village.

➕ Off map to southwest

YANKEE STADIUM

www.yankees.mlb.com

If you want to see what makes the New Yorker tick, go see a Yankees home game. The Yankees dominated the early era of baseball. In 1920 Babe Ruth joined the team and quickly became a hero. The team clinched the World Series title in 1996, 1998, 1999, 2000 and 2009, the year they moved into their new Yankee Stadium.

➕ Off map to north ✉ E 161st Street, Bronx ☎ 718/293-4300 🕐 Season runs Apr–Oct. Check schedule for games 🍴 Concession stands 🚇 4, B, D 161st Street/Yankee Stadium 🎫 Expensive

The Yankee Stadium in the Bronx, home of the New York Yankees

City Tours

This section contains self-guided tours that will help you explore the sights in each of the city's regions. Each tour is designed to take a day, with a map pinpointing the recommended places along the way. There is a quick reference guide at the end of each tour, listing everything you need in that region, so you know exactly what's close by.

CITY TOURS

Lower Manhattan

The cradle of New York, Lower Manhattan has bags of history—new immigrants landed here from the 17th century until the early 20th century—as well as the Financial District, historic Seaport and fashionable SoHo.

Morning
Start the day at the tip of Manhattan in **Battery Park** (▷ 66), with its splendid views of New York Harbor. Ferries for the **Statue of Liberty** (▷ 56–57) and **Ellis Island** (▷ 28–29) leave from Castle Clinton, but save these for a separate day. Cross State Street to admire the beautiful Beaux Arts facade of the **U.S. Custom House** (▷ 73), housing the National Museum of the American Indian. Then proceed along **Bowling Green**, the small square opposite, past the Charging Bull statue (right), a symbol of Wall Street.

Mid-morning
Walk up Broadway and note the plaques embedded in the pavement commemorating historic events that have been honored by ticker-tape parades. **Trinity Church** (left; ▷ 61) marks the west end of **Wall Street** (▷ 60–61); stroll around the old churchyard, then head down Wall Street to **Federal Hall**, the **New York Stock Exchange** and other sites.

Lunch
Rub shoulders with Financial District workers and have a pub lunch at **The Bailey Pub & Brasserie** (▷ 142), one block north of Wall Street. The steak frites is delicious, or try a hearty *plat du jour* such as shepherd's pie.

Afternoon
Walk north on Front Street to **South Street Seaport** (▷ 54–55). From the waterfront along the East River there are good views of **Brooklyn Bridge** (▷ 66). Follow Dover Street east to **City Hall** (▷ 67), then take Centre Street north into **Chinatown** (▷ 20–21). Explore its bustling markets, its quiet temples and herbalist shops. If you're baffled by the many shops selling Chinese wares, **Pearl River Mart** (▷ 122) has everything you could wish for under one roof.

Mid-afternoon
Chinatown spills north into **Little Italy**. Walk north on Mulberry Street, past the **Italian American Museum** (▷ 68), and when you reach **St. Patrick's Old Cathedral** (▷ 72), turn left on Prince Street, which will bring you into **SoHo** (▷ 52–53). Grab a coffee at **Dean & DeLuca** (▷ 52) to keep you going as you browse the art galleries, ogle the cast-iron buildings and indulge in some shopping. Most stores here stay open into early evening.

Evening
There are plenty of ultra-chic bars in SoHo for a cocktail or a nightcap. For some old SoHo atmosphere, try **Fanelli's** (94 Prince Street, between Mercer and Greene streets, tel 212/226-9412).

Dinner
Nolita (North of Little Italy), which borders SoHo to the east, has become the latest dining hot spot in Lower Manhattan. Yet this neighborhood still retains its low-key ambience. **Travertine** (▷ 149), set in a historic building, stands out for its innovative Italian dishes, sleek decor, and snazzy cocktail bar. Be sure to save room for the chocolate pudding dessert.

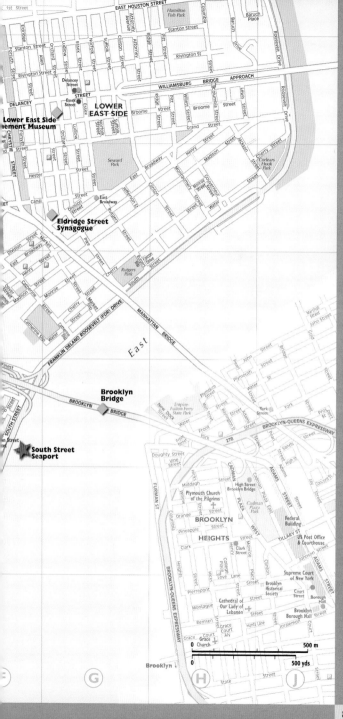

Lower Manhattan Quick Reference Guide

 TOP 25

 SIGHTS AND EXPERIENCES

Chinatown (▷ 20)
Explore another world in this bustling neighborhood of street-side produce stalls, herbalist shops, Buddhist temples, dim sum parlors and Chinese restaurants.

Ellis Island (▷ 28)
Follow in the footsteps of millions of immigrants who passed through this gateway to New York and the New World, and hear their stories in the exhibits and artifacts.

SoHo (▷ 52)
The historic district South of Houston features leading art galleries, trendy boutiques, top fashion chains, cool bars and restaurants in 19th-century cast-iron buildings.

South Street Seaport (▷ 54)
While the shops, restaurants and bars lining the cobbled streets and piers are undoubtedly touristy, this is one of New York's oldest and most important historic districts.

Statue of Liberty (▷ 56)
A visit to New York's—and America's—most iconic landmark is a must. The ferry ride to the island is impressive, as is the view from the statue's crown.

Wall Street (▷ 60)
During Dutch colonial times, Wall Street marked the northern boundary of New York. Now home to brokers and bankers, it's the powerhouse of the US economy.

Downtown and Chelsea

The Downtown area from 30th Street south to Houston Street encompasses Greenwich Village with its brownstones and artsy vibe; bohemian East Village; the Meatpacking District with its bars and designer stores; and Chelsea, packed with art.

Morning

Start the day in **Union Square** (right; ▷ 72), preferably on a Monday, Wednesday, Friday or Saturday, when you can browse the food stalls of **Union Square Greenmarket** and pick up a coffee and pastry for breakfast on the go. Head south on Broadway, past lovely **Grace Church** (▷ 68), then turn left on any street into the **East Village** (▷ 26–27). There are no must-see sights here, but plenty of atmosphere, especially along the bohemian stretch of **St. Mark's Place** (E 8th Street), with funky shops, record stores, ethnic restaurants and alternative arts venues.

Mid-morning/lunch

Downtown neighborhoods are so full of tempting eateries that it's better to graze your way through this tour than stop for a full-blown lunch. **Veselka** (▷ 149) is a great place to absorb the East Village's Ukrainian heritage along with delicious *blintzes* (pancakes) and *pierogis* (dumplings). Walk west on E Ninth Street (or take the M8 bus) to Fifth Avenue. Then head south to the start of this famous thoroughfare at **Washington Square** (▷ 73).

Afternoon

Walk through the square into the heart of **Greenwich Village** (▷ 38–39). This is a prime place for people-watching, and you could spend days exploring the one-of-a-kind shops and cafés. Grab an authentic New York slice at **Joe's Pizza** (7 Carmine Street at 6th Avenue). Stroll the pretty residential streets around Bedford, Grove and Barrow streets in the **West Village**. Then head north on Greenwich Street to the **Meatpacking District** (▷ 69).

Mid-afternoon

After checking out the designer stores, walk north on the **High Line** (▷ 68), the elevated promenade, for views over Chelsea and the Hudson River. Descend at 16th Street to grab a snack at **Chelsea Market** (left; ▷ 121), then continue along the High Line. From the end of the High Line at 20th Street, you're a stone's throw from the **Chelsea Art District** (▷ 66–67).

Evening

Walk along W 23rd Street past the **Chelsea Hotel** (▷ 66) . At the 7th Avenue subway stop, take Line 1 downtown to Christopher Street/Sheridan Square, back in Greenwich Village. For a historic watering hole, head for the **White Horse Tavern** (▷ 137) on Hudson Street, where poet Dylan Thomas drank his last.

Dinner

The bistro-style **North Square restaurant** (▷ 147) at the **Washington Square Hotel** (▷ 159) is a good choice for superb Mediterranean dishes accompanied by an award-winning wine list.

Late evening

After dinner, you're well placed for whatever musical entertainment takes your fancy. For cool jazz, head for the **Blue Note** (▷ 132) or the renowned **Village Vanguard** (178 7th Avenue South at W 11th Street, tel 212/255-4037). You could also check out the live music bars on Macdougal and Bleecker streets. Alternatively take a taxi to the night-clubs of the **Meatpacking District** (right; ▷ 69).

West 38th Street
West 37th Street
West 38th Street
West 37th Street
West 36th Street
West 35th Street

12
Jacob K Javits Convention Center

DYER AVENUE
West 34th Street
West 33rd Street

WEST 34TH STREET
West 33rd Street
West 32nd Street
West 31st Street

34th Street Penn Station
34th Street Penn Station
34th Street Herald Square

Macy's
WEST 34TH STREET
West 33rd Street

Madison Square Garden
Pennsylvania Station
West 32nd Street
West 31st Street

13
WEST 30TH STREET
West 29th Street
West 28th Street
West 28th Street

11TH AVENUE
10TH AVENUE
9TH AVENUE
8TH AVENUE
7TH AVENUE
AVENUE OF THE AMERICAS (6TH AVENUE)

West 30th Street
West 29th Street
28th Street

Chelsea Park
West 27th Street
West 26th Street
West 25th Street

CHELSEA ART DISTRICT

Chelsea Waterside Park

14
West 24th Street
West 23rd Street
West 22nd Street

23rd Street
23rd Street
23rd Street

West 24th Street
West 23rd Street
West 22nd Street

West 21st Street
West 20th Street
West 19th Street
West 18th Street
West 17th Street

CHELSEA

18th Street

West 21st Street
West 20th Street
West 19th Street
West 18th Street

Rubin Museum of Art

West 17th
West 16th

15
West 16th Street
West 15th Street

Chelsea Market

14th Street
8th Avenue
14th Street

14th Street

WEST 14TH STREET

WEST 14th

6th Avenue
WEST 14th

West 13th Street

Meatpacking District

Village Vanguard

Jefferson Market Library

16
Hudson

High Line

White Horse Tavern

GREENWICH VILLAGE

Christopher Street Sheridan Square

Church of St Luke-in-the-Fields

Non Square Restaura

Blu Not

Joe's Pizza

West 4th St-Washington Square

17
Bleecker

Saint Luke's Pl
J J Walker Park

HOUSTON
Houston Street

New York City Fire Department Museum

18
Spring Street

(B)   (C)   (D)

Downtown and Chelsea
Quick Reference Guide

East Village (▷ 26)

It's well worth exploring this Downtown "village." Its residential streets house a vibrant mix of young families, Eastern European immigrants and latter-day bohemians, interspersed with avant-garde fashion and music shops, ethnic restaurants and theaters. Home to New York's grandest families in the first half of the 19th century, it also has several graceful churches and notable public buildings.

Greenwich Village (▷ 38)

Few neighborhoods in New York are as famous as leafy Greenwich Village with its fine brownstones. Its coffee houses nurtured the Beatnik generation in the 1950s, its music bars launched Bob Dylan, Joan Baez and other folk music heroes of the 1960s, and by the 1970s Christopher Street had become the center of the gay rights movement. The Village's jazz clubs are world-renowned.

MORE TO SEE   64

Chelsea
Flatiron Building
Grace Church
High Line
Meatpacking District
Rubin Museum of Art
Union Square
Washington Square

SHOP — 114

Accessories
Village Tannery
Clothes
Cynthia Rowley
Hotoveli
Jeffrey New York
Marc Jacobs
Scoop
Discount
DSW and Filene's

Loehmann's
Food and Wine
Chelsea Market
Union Square Greenmarket
Homewares
ABC Carpet and Home
Shoes
DSW and Filene's

ENTERTAINMENT — 126

Bars
McSorley's Old Ale House
Pete's Tavern
Vintage Irving
White Horse Tavern
Cabaret/Burlesque
Duplex (▷ panel, 134)
Joe's Pub
Lips (▷ panel, 134)
Clubs
Café Wha?

Comedy
Gotham Comedy Club
Jazz
Blue Note
Karaoke
Sing Sing Karaoke
Live Music
Mercury Lounge
Theater/Performance
PS 122

EAT — 138

Asian
Almond
Yama (▷ panel, 144)
Contemporary
Gotham Bar and Grill
North Square
The Spotted Pig

Italian
Del Posto
Mexican
Mary Ann's
Polish/Ukrainian
Veselka

The High Line, an elevated walkway created from an old freight railroad

Midtown

Midtown is a must for visitors. It has leading museums, pulsating Times Square, Grand Central Terminal plus the magnet for shoppers—Fifth Avenue. It also has three of New York's most famous skyscrapers, two with observatories, and the views are stupendous.

Morning

Get an early start at **Rockefeller Center** (▷ 50–51). The subway concourse below the GE Building and surrounding the plaza is full of restaurants; pick up a coffee and pastry at **Au Bon Pain**, or have a more substantial breakfast at the **Rock Center Cafe**, which looks out on the famous ice rink. Be sure to see the many beautiful artworks around the complex, before or after whisking to the observation decks at **Top of the Rock** (right) for majestic morning views over Manhattan.

Mid-morning

Walk west along 50th Street to Radio City Music Hall, and turn right up Sixth Avenue. Turn right on 53rd Street to visit the **Museum of Modern Art** (▷ 46–47).

Lunch

"Quick" and "inexpensive" are foreign words in this part of Midtown. Your best bet for a simple lunch that won't break the bank is to grab a bite at one of MoMA's cafés. Or if you're dying for a delicious deli sandwich, there are two good options close by: **Stage Deli** (834 7th Avenue between 53rd and 54th streets) and **Carnegie Deli** (854 7th Avenue at 55th Street).

Afternoon

Walk east to **Fifth Avenue** (▷ 32–33) and let the shopping spree begin—even if you're just window shopping and ogling the fabulous displays. If you enter only one store, make it **Saks Fifth Avenue** (▷ 124); the perfume and cosmetic counters fill the ground floor. As you head south, you'll pass beautiful **St. Patrick's Cathedral** (▷ 71).

Mid-afternoon
Turn left on E 45th Street and walk to the Park Avenue entrance of **Grand Central Terminal** (▷ 36–37). Admire its stunning main concourse, then head downstairs for a welcome rest and a snack in the **Food Court** (▷ 145). Exit on 42nd Street, and detour one block east to step into the art deco lobby of the **Chrysler Building** (▷ 22–23). Then walk west on 42nd Street to Fifth Avenue, and visit the **New York Public Library** (left; ▷ 48–49).

Evening
As dusk falls, continue west and turn right up Broadway into **Times Square** (▷ 58–59), in all its neon glory. Head for the **TKTS booth** (▷ 58), where you may get a discount ticket for a Broadway show.

Dinner
Times Square is notorious for chain restaurants, but a good choice for real New York fare is **John's** (▷ 146). There's also a branch of **Carmine's** (▷ 144) at 200 W 44th Street, off Times Square.

Late evening
Afterwards, take in that Broadway show, and/or grab a cab to end the evening with the best nightcap of all: the view of the twinkling lights of Manhattan from the top of the **Empire State Building** (right; ▷ 30–31).

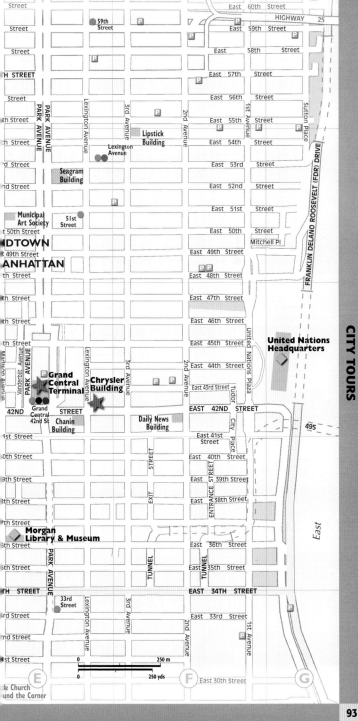

Street

Street

Street

Street

H STREET

Street

th Street

h Street

'd Street

nd Street

Municipal
Art Society

t 50th Street

DTOWN

t 49th Street

ANHATTAN

th Street

th Street

th Street

th Street

th Street

42ND

1st Street

0th Street

9th Street

8th Street

7th Street

5th Street

5th Street

H STREET

rd Street

nd Street

st Street

le Church
und the Corner

East 60th Street

HIGHWAY 25

East 59th Street

East 58th Street

East 57th Street

East 56th Street

East 55th Street

East 54th

East 53rd Street

East 52nd Street

East 51st Street

East 50th Street

East 49th Street

East 48th Street

East 47th Street

East 46th Street

East 45th Street

East 44th Street

East 43rd Street

EAST 42ND STREET

East 41st
Street

East 40th Street

East 39th Street

East 38th Street

East 36th Street

East 35th Street

EAST 34TH STREET

East 33rd Street

East 30th Street

59th
Street

Lipstick
Building

Seagram
Building

Lexington
Avenue

51st
Street

**Grand
Central
Terminal**

**Chrysler
Building**

Grand
Central
42nd St

STREET

Chanin
Building

Daily News
Building

**Morgan
Library & Museum**

33rd
Street

**United Nations
Headquarters**

Sutton Place

FRANKLIN DELANO ROOSEVELT (FDR) DRIVE

Mitchell Pl

United Nations Plaza

Tudor

City
Place

495

East

Park Avenue

Lexington Avenue

3rd Avenue

2nd Avenue

1st Avenue

Vanderbilt Avenue

Madison Avenue

Park Avenue

STREET

EXIT

ENTRANCE STREET

TUNNEL

TUNNEL

| 0 | 250 m |
| 0 | 250 yds |

E

F

G

Midtown Quick Reference Guide

 SIGHTS AND EXPERIENCES

Chrysler Building (▷ 22)
New York's best-loved skyscraper symbolizes the stylishness of the art deco age.

Empire State Building (▷ 30)
The most famous New York sky-scraper affords panoramic views over Manhattan by day or night.

Fifth Avenue (▷ 32)
For high fashion, style and quality, there's no better place to shop than Fifth Avenue.

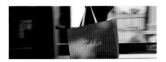

Grand Central Terminal (▷ 36)
Some half a million people pass through this stunning Beaux Arts concourse every day.

Museum of Modern Art (▷ 46)
From 19th-century masterpieces to contemporary, this is one of the city's leading art museums.

New York Public Library (▷ 48)
See the fine carved ceiling and the glorious reading rooms of this Beaux Arts landmark.

Rockefeller Center (▷ 50)
Admire the plaza and artworks of this urban complex, then take in the view from the Top of the Rock.

Times Square (▷ 58)
Come here at night to see the blitz of neon at the heart of New York's famous Theater District.

MORE TO SEE 64

International Center of Photography
Morgan Library & Museum
Paley Center for Media
St. Patrick's Cathedral
Trump Tower
United Nations Headquarters

SHOP 114

Department Stores
Bergdorf Goodman
Macy's
Saks Fifth Avenue
Food and Wine
Whole Foods Market
  (▷ panel, 120)
Homewares
Michael C. Fina

Shoes
Manolo Blahnik
Sports Goods
Nike Town NY
Technology
Apple Store
Toys
FAO Schwarz

ENTERTAINMENT 126

Bars
Empire Hotel Rooftop Bar
Four Seasons Hotel
Classical Music
Carnegie Hall
Comedy
The Laurie Beechman Theatre
Jazz
Birdland

Live Music
Best Buy Theater
Madison Square Garden
Theater/Performance
The New Victory Theater
New World Stages
Radio City Music Hall
TV Show Recording
The Late Show with David
  Letterman

EAT 138

Casual
Grand Central Terminal Food Court
John's
Classic NY
'21' Club
Four Seasons
Oyster Bar

Contemporary
Le Bernardin
Casa Lever
Per Se
European
Uncle Nick's

Upper East Side and Central Park

Central Park is a huge green space for all Manhattan. The museums of the Upper East Side, facing the park along Fifth Avenue, are renowned worldwide. Their collections range from priceless antiquities to modern art, design, ethnic culture and history.

Morning
It's unlikely you'll visit more than two museums in a day. This tour will take you past the most popular, and give you a taste of Central Park in between. Most museums don't open until 10 (9.30 for the Met), so start with an early morning stroll in **Central Park** (left; ▷ 18–19). Enter at the southeast corner by Grand Army Plaza (E 59th Street and 5th Avenue). Follow the wide, paved road north into the park. Footpaths lead down to The Pond, with lovely views of the city skyline. You'll pass the Zoo on your way to the Dairy Visitor Center, where you can pick up a park map. Continue north along The Mall, lined with one of the largest stands of elm trees in America. The southern end, Literary Walk, has statues of famous writers.

Mid-morning
Just before the Naumburg Bandshell, veer right and follow paths to exit the park at 69th Street. Go one block north to visit the **Frick Collection** (▷ 34–35). Otherwise, continue through the park to the Bethesda Terrace and Fountain (right), overlooking the Lake. Admire the view, then take the pedestrian walkway beneath the terrace—look up to see the Minton tile ceiling. Follow the lakeside path to your right. At Loeb Boathouse veer right to Conservatory Water, the pretty model boat pond. Exit the park further on at 76th Street to visit the **Whitney Museum of American Art** (▷ 62–63).

Lunch

The Met, Whitney, Guggenheim, Cooper-Hewitt and Neue Galerie all have cafés. In Central Park, the **Loeb Boathouse Restaurant** (▷ 147) has an express café as well as formal dining on the terrace. Alternatively picnic on the Great Lawn behind the Met.

Afternoon

Even if you only have a couple of hours, a visit to the **Metropolitan Museum of Art** (left; ▷ 44–45) is well worthwhile. It stands right in Central Park. Try to catch a free museum highlights tour (times vary). At Fifth Avenue and 86th Street is the **Neue Galerie** (▷ 70). Further north at 89th Street is the **Guggenheim Museum** (▷ 40–41), housed in Frank Lloyd Wright's stunning circular building. Beyond is the **Cooper-Hewitt National Design Museum** (▷ 24–25) and the **Jewish Museum** (▷ 69). All of these face Central Park's massive Reservoir. The running track and bridle path around the Reservoir are good places to stroll.

Evening

It's not a good idea to walk in Central Park after dark, so unless your chosen museum has a late-night opening, head for the Carlyle Hotel and have a cocktail in **Bemelman's Bar** (▷ 132).

Dinner

The superb cuisine at nearby **Café Boulud** (▷ 143) makes it a good choice for dinner.

Late evening

Return to Carlyle Hotel's **Café Carlyle** (▷ 132) for jazz and cabaret.

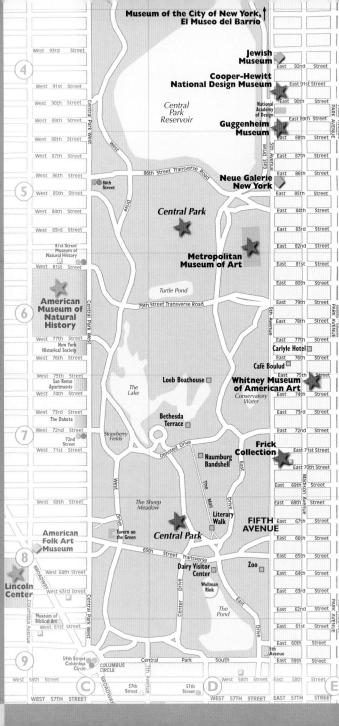

Museum of the City of New York,↑
El Museo del Barrio

West 93rd Street

Jewish Museum
East 92nd Street

Cooper-Hewitt National Design Museum
East 91st Street

West 91st Street

West 90th Street
East 90th Street

National Academy of Design

West 89th Street
East 89th Street

Central Park Reservoir

Guggenheim Museum
East 88th Street

West 88th Street
East 87th Street

West 87th Street
East 86th Street

West 86th Street
86th Street Transverse Road

Neue Galerie New York
East 86th Street

86th Street

West 85th Street
East 85th Street

West 84th Street
East 84th Street

Central Park

West 83rd Street
East 83rd Street

West 82nd Street

Metropolitan Museum of Art
East 81st Street

81st Street Museum of Natural History

West 81st Street
East 80th Street

Turtle Pond

East 79th Street

79th Street Transverse Road

American Museum of Natural History

East 78th Street

West 77th Street
New York Historical Society

East 77th Street

West 76th Street
Carlyle Hotel

Café Boulud
East 76th Street

West 75th Street
San Remo Apartments

Whitney Museum of American Art
East 75th Street

West 74th Street

Loeb Boathouse

Conservatory Water
East 74th Street

West 73rd Street
The Dakota
East 73rd Street

The Lake

West 72nd Street
East 72nd Street

72nd Street

Bethesda Terrace

Frick Collection
East 71st Street

West 71st Street

Strawberry Fields

Olmsted Drive

Naumburg Bandshell
East 70th Street

East 69th Street

West 68th Street
East 68th Street

The Sheep Meadow

Literary Walk

FIFTH AVENUE
East 67th Street

American Folk Art Museum

Tavern on the Green

Central Park
East 66th Street

West 64th Street
65th Street Transverse

East 65th Street

Lincoln Center

Dairy Visitor Center

Zoo
East 64th Street

West 63rd Street
East 63rd Street

Wollman Rink

Museum of Biblical Art
West 61st Street

The Pond
East 62nd Street

East 61st Street

East 60th Street

59th Street Columbus Circle

COLUMBUS CIRCLE

Central Park South

Fifth Avenue
East 59th Street

West 58th Street
West 58th Street
East 58th Street

WEST 57TH STREET
57th Street
57th Street
WEST 57TH STREET
EAST 57TH STREET

Upper East Side and Central Park
Quick Reference Guide

 SIGHTS AND EXPERIENCES

Central Park (▷ 18)
This great, green space is a vision-ary creation in the heart of the city. Join New Yorkers as they walk, jog, cycle, row, picnic, play ball and escape the urban buzz.

Cooper-Hewitt National Design Museum (▷ 24)
If it has reopened following refur-bishment, browse the collections of furniture and decorative arts in the sumptuous Carnegie mansion.

Frick Collection (▷ 34)
The mansion of this 19th-century robber baron is worth a visit in itself, and forms a splendid back-drop for his magnificent collection of old masters and decorative arts.

Guggenheim Museum (▷ 40)
Frank Lloyd Wright's ground-breaking, nautilus-shaped building gets all the glory, but the collection of late19th- and 20th-century art is also superb.

Metropolitan Museum of Art (▷ 44)
Don't be daunted by the size of this fabulous art museum. Viewing just one or two of its collections will leave lasting memories.

Whitney Museum of American Art (▷ 62)
The great American artists of the 20th century form the core collec-tion, while its Biennial is a hot New York event.

CITY TOURS

Upper West Side

West of Central Park is a largely residential, pleasantly leafy neighborhood of grand apartment buildings and big brownstones. Its major attractions are Lincoln Center and the wonderful American Museum of Natural History.

Morning
Start the tour at **Lincoln Center** (▷ 42–43). Walk around the plaza, admiring the Revson Fountain, the Metropolitan Opera House and other cultural venues. Guided tours are available if you want to go behind the scenes; they leave from the David Rubenstein Atrium. From the northeast corner of the Lincoln Center, cross over the intersection with Broadway to the **American Folk Art Museum** (left; ▷ 66). Continue up Columbus Avenue, taking in its shops and restaurants. If you're ready for a snack, you'll pass the **Magnolia Bakery** (200 Columbus Avenue)— it's never too early for one of their cupcakes.

Mid-morning
Turn right on W 72nd Street. On the corner with Central Park West is the Dakota, the first luxury co-op apartment building on the Upper West Side. Its most famous resident, John Lennon, was shot outside the south gate in 1980. Cross the road to enter **Central Park** (▷ 18–19), and follow the path to Strawberry Fields, where the *Imagine* mosaic (right) is the centerpoint of a memorial peace garden. From here there is a good view of the Dakota and the towers of the neighboring San Remo Apartments. Further on is the **New York Historical Society** (170 Central Park West; www.nyhistory.org), in one of the nation's last Beaux Arts buildings. Cross back to Central Park West and continue on 73rd Street to Broadway.

Lunch

Broadway is another great shopping street. Continue north to 80th Street, where you can put together a picnic from the gourmet fare at **Zabar's** (right; ▷ 125), or get a sandwich at their adjoining café. Take it to **Riverside Park**, two blocks west, with views over the Hudson River.

Afternoon

Plan to spend the entire afternoon at the **American Museum of Natural History** (▷ 14–15). Between the dinosaur halls, the animal dioramas, the Rose Center for Earth and Space (left), and much more, you won't see it all.

Dinner

You won't have too much further to walk for an early dinner at **Ouest** (▷ 148). Sink into the red leather booths and enjoy the inspired cuisine of Tom Valenti, one of New York's favorite chefs.

Evening

The No. 1 subway is not far away for a quick ride back to **Lincoln Center** (right). Even if you haven't got tickets for an evening performance, a walk through the lit-up plaza is a magical way to end the day.

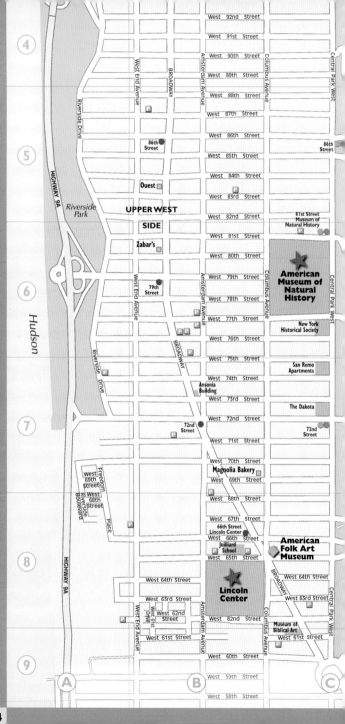

Hudson

West 92nd Street
West 91st Street
West 90th Street
West 89th Street
West 88th Street
West 87th Street
West 86th Street
West 85th Street
West 84th Street
West 83rd Street
West 82nd Street
West 81st Street
West 80th Street
West 79th Street
West 78th Street
West 77th Street
West 76th Street
West 75th Street
West 74th Street
West 73rd Street
West 72nd Street
West 71st Street
West 70th Street
West 69th Street
West 68th Street
West 67th Street
West 66th Street
West 65th Street
West 64th Street
West 63rd Street
West 62nd Street
West 61st Street
West 60th Street
West 59th Street
West 58th Street

Riverside Drive

West End Avenue

BROADWAY

Amsterdam Avenue

Columbus Avenue

Central Park West

HIGHWAY 9A

Riverside Park

86th Street

Ouest

UPPER WEST

SIDE

Zabar's

79th Street

72nd Street

Freedom Place

Riverside Boulevard

West 69th Street

West 68th Street

Magnolia Bakery

66th Street Lincoln Center

Juilliard School

Lincoln Center

Riverside Drive

West End Avenue

West 64th Street

West 63rd Street

West 62nd Street

West 61st Street

Amsterdam Avenue

Columbus Avenue

81st Street Museum of Natural History

American Museum of Natural History

New York Historical Society

San Remo Apartments

The Dakota

72nd Street

American Folk Art Museum

BROADWAY

Museum of Biblical Art

West 64th Street

West 63rd Street

West 61st Street

Central Park West

Ansonia Building

86th Street

72nd Street

4
5
6
7
8
9

A
B
C

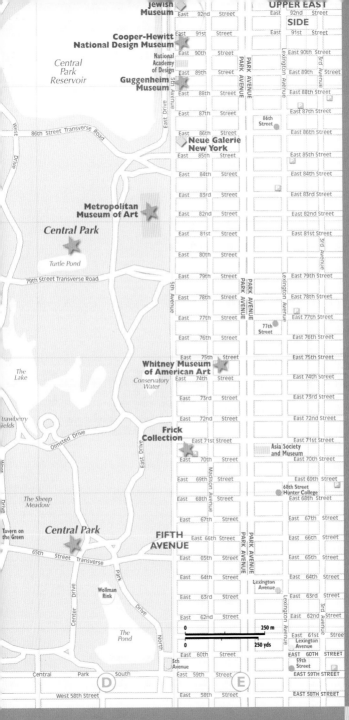

Jewish Museum

UPPER EAST

East 92nd Street   East 92nd Street

SIDE

Cooper-Hewitt
National Design Museum

East 91st Street   East 91st Street

East 90th Street   East 90th Street

Central
Park
Reservoir

National
Academy
of Design

East 89th Street   East 89th Street

Guggenheim
Museum

East 88th Street   East 88th Street

East 87th Street   East 87th Street

86th
Street

86th Street Transverse Road

East 86th Street   East 86th Street

Neue Galerie
New York

East 85th Street   East 85th Street

East 84th Street   East 84th Street

East 83rd Street   East 83rd Street

Metropolitan
Museum of Art

East 82nd Street   East 82nd Street

Central Park

East 81st Street   East 81st Street

East 80th Street

Turtle Pond

79th Street Transverse Road

East 79th Street   East 79th Street

East 78th Street   East 78th Street

East 77th Street   East 77th Street

77th
Street

East 76th Street   East 76th Street

East 75th Street   East 75th Street

The
Lake

Whitney Museum
of American Art

Conservatory
Water

East 74th Street   East 74th Street

East 73rd Street   East 73rd Street

Strawberry
Fields

East 72nd Street   East 72nd Street

Olmsted Drive

Frick
Collection

East 71st Street   East 71st Street

East 70th Street

Asia Society
and Museum

East 70th Street

East 69th Street   East 69th Street

68th Street
Hunter College

The Sheep
Meadow

East 68th Street   East 68th Street

East 67th Street   East 67th Street

Tavern on
the Green

Central Park

FIFTH
AVENUE

East 66th Street   East 66th Street

65th Street Transverse

East 65th Street   East 65th Street

East 64th Street   East 64th Street

Wollman
Rink

East 63rd Street   East 63rd Street

Lexington
Avenue

East 62nd Street   East 62nd Street

The
Pond

0   250 m

0   250 yds

East 61st Stree
Lexington
Avenue

East 60th Street   EAST 60TH STREET

5th
Avenue

59th
Street

Central   Park   South   East 59th Street   EAST 59TH STREET

West 58th Street   East 58th Street   EAST 58TH STREET

D   **E**

CITY TOURS

Upper West Side Quick Reference Guide

 SIGHTS AND EXPERIENCES

American Museum of Natural History (▷ 14)

This is the largest natural history museum in the world. The lifesize, rearing Barosaurus in the main entrance hall is a clue to the renowned dinosaur halls, where fossil specimens of some of the earliest dinosaur discoveries are displayed. Add to that a priceless collection of gemstones, animal dioramas, the Rose Center for Earth and Space with its amazing planetarium, and more, and you could easily spend a day here.

Lincoln Center (▷ 42)

New York's premier performing arts complex is a sight to behold, with its gushing fountains and gleaming buildings, the huge arched windows and chandeliers of the Metropolitan Opera House, and the glowing lights reflected in its wide central plaza. In addition to housing the Metropolitan Opera, it is home to the New York Philharmonic, the Juilliard School of Music, the New York City Ballet and many others, and offers a vast array of entertainment.

MORE TO SEE	64

American Folk Art Museum

CITY TOURS

View of the Dakota (middle) and San Remo apartments (right) from Central Park

Further Afield

New York's outer boroughs are increasingly attractive to those who seek a more relaxed approach to life. Brooklyn (▷ 16–17) especially has plenty to engage visitors. With an early start, you can take in its top sights as well as two classic New York experiences.

Morning

Join the city's commuters and begin your day at the tip of Manhattan at the Staten Island Ferry Terminal. Of course, you'll be heading in the opposite direction, but no matter. The ferry ride (right) across Upper New York Bay is stunning in both directions, and even better, it's free. It's worth waiting for one of the old orange ferries, which have outside decks to give you a better view of the Statue of Liberty—visible from the right side of the boat on the way out—and other sights. The round trip to and from **Staten Island** (▷ 75) takes an hour; when you arrive you can catch the next ferry back to Manhattan.

Mid-morning

Disembark and walk up Broadway to Bowling Green, where you can catch the No. 4 or 5 subway train to the Brooklyn Bridge/City Hall stop. On Park Row, a sidewalk entrance leads up to the wooden walkway of **Brooklyn Bridge** (left; ▷ 66). A walk (or jog) across the bridge is a must, and New Yorkers love it as much as visitors do. It's about a 20-minute walk, though it can take twice as long with stops to admire the views back to the Manhattan skyline.

Lunch

When you come to the end of the bridge, you'll have worked up an appetite, so when you see the DUMBO sign, take the stairwell down to the street and head towards the water. **Grimaldi's** (▷ 145) on Old Fulton Street has some of the best pizza in New York. Afterwards, walk along the promenade for splendid vistas across the river to Manhattan.

Afternoon

Walk through the pretty brownstone-lined streets of Brooklyn Heights to the Clark Street subway stop, and take Line 2 or 3 to the Eastern Parkway stop. This eastern side of Prospect Park contains two of Brooklyn's finest attractions: the **Brooklyn Museum of Art** (right; ▷ 16), and **Brooklyn Botanic Garden** (900 Washington Avenue, tel 718/623-7200), with its rose garden, bonsai museum and Japanese Hill-and-Pond Garden. A visit to either could easily take up the rest of the afternoon.

Dinner

From the western side of Prospect Park, walk down through the lovely Park Slope neighborhood, which is filled with attractive brownstones. Follow First Street to Fifth Avenue, where the **Blue Ribbon restaurant** (▷ 143) has a raw bar and is renowned for it excellent choice of fresh seafood dishes.

Late evening

To sample some Brooklyn nightlife, walk four blocks north on Fifth Avenue to **Union Hall** (702 Union Street, tel 718/638-4400). This converted warehouse has a tasteful library lounge, two indoor bocce ball courts, and a bar and live music venue downstairs. From the nearby Union Street subway stop you can catch the R train back to Manhattan.

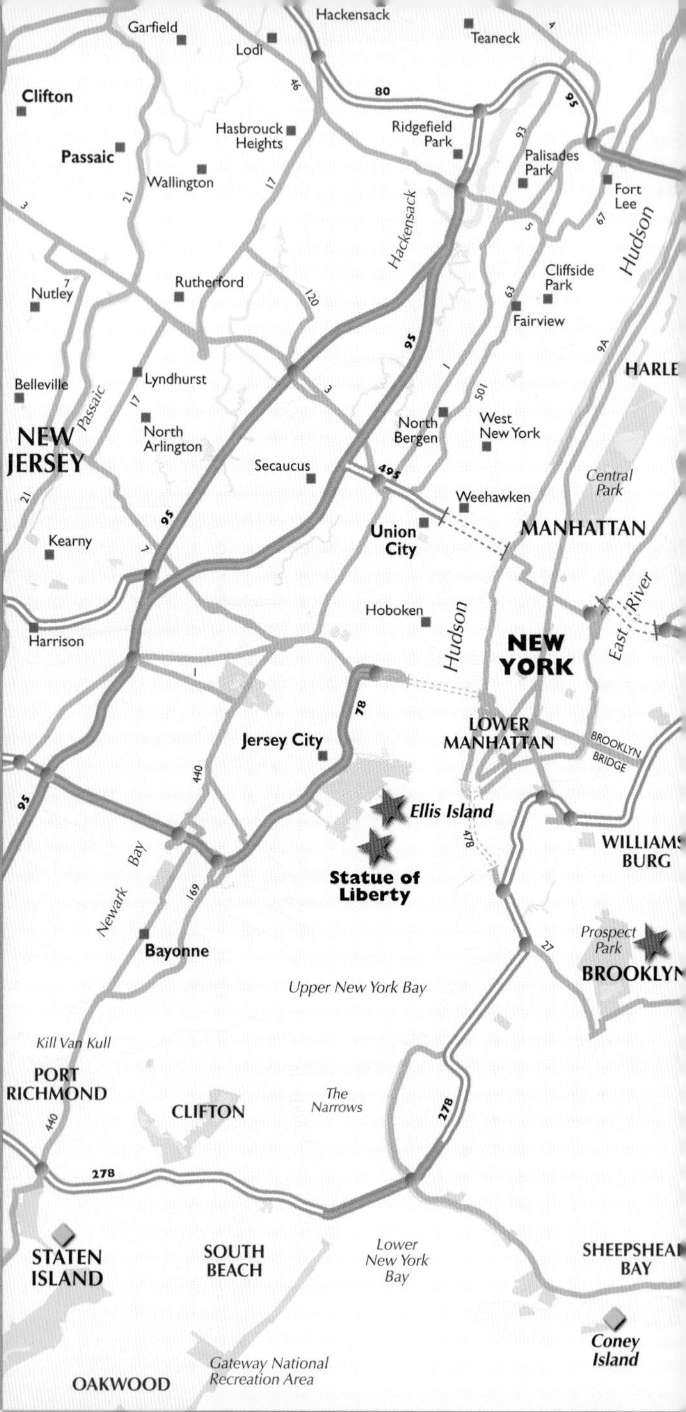

Garfield
Hackensack
Lodi
Teaneck
Clifton
Hasbrouck Heights
Ridgefield Park
80
95
Passaic
Wallington
93
Palisades Park
Fort Lee
21
17
Hudson
46
Nutley
Rutherford
Hackensack
Cliffside Park
Belleville
Lyndhurst
120
Fairview
95
9A
HARLE
NEW JERSEY
North Arlington
501
North Bergen
West New York
Central Park
Secaucus
495
Passaic
Weehawken
MANHATTAN
Kearny
95
Union City
Hoboken
Harrison
Hudson
NEW YORK
East River
Jersey City
78
LOWER MANHATTAN
BROOKLYN BRIDGE
440
Ellis Island
478
WILLIAMS BURG
169
Statue of Liberty
Prospect Park
95
Bayonne
27
BROOKLYN
Newark Bay
Upper New York Bay
Kill Van Kull
PORT RICHMOND
The Narrows
440
CLIFTON
278
SHEEPSHEAD BAY
278
STATEN ISLAND
SOUTH BEACH
Lower New York Bay
Coney Island
OAKWOOD
Gateway National Recreation Area

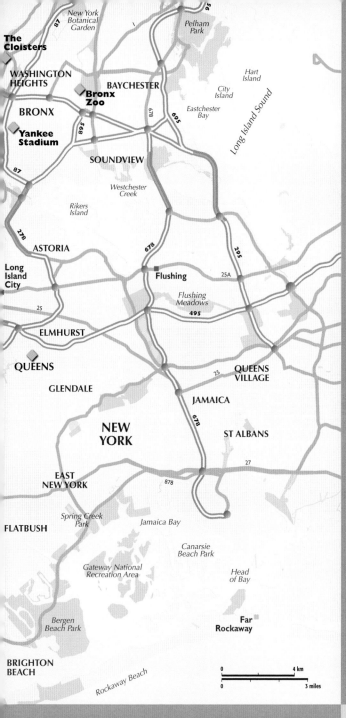

SIGHTS AND EXPERIENCES

Brooklyn (▷ 16–17)

If you've ever wondered what New York is like beyond Manhattan, Brooklyn is the best place to start. Neighborhoods in Brooklyn Heights and Park Slope are lined with classic brownstones and have a thriving restaurant scene. In Prospect Park, the Brooklyn Museum of Art contains a renowned Egyptian collection and the Sackler Center for Feminist Art. Alongside is the Brooklyn Botanic Garden. Walk back to Manhattan across the Brooklyn Bridge—a classic New York experience.

MORE TO SEE	64

Bronx Zoo
The Cloisters
Coney Island
Queens
Staten Island
Yankee Stadium

EAT	138

Casual
Grimaldi's
Classic NY
Peter Luger
Contemporary
Blue Ribbon

Grocery
Henry's End
River Café
Sherwood Café (▷ panel, 148)

1920
THE WONDER WHEEL,
A 150 FOOT TALL FERRIS WHEEL
OPENS AT CONEY ISLAND.

Shop

Whether you're looking for the best local products, a department store or a quirky boutique, you'll find them all in New York. In this section shops are listed alphabetically.

SHOP

Introduction

Thought there was nothing you couldn't buy over the internet? Think again! New York is a shopping heaven, with clothing, furniture, food and souvenirs available no place else. Shopping is still one of the best ways to get an inside look at life in New York—its trends, pace, cultural influences and sense of humor. From massive department stores to small boutiques, the city has something for everyone.

A Piece of New York

You'll find all kinds of NYC paraphernalia—from Statue of Liberty coin banks and taxicab neckties to sweatshirts bearing the New York Police Department initials and Yankee baseball caps. Museum shops sell reproductions, posters, jewelry, stationery and commemorative items.

Fashion

For fashion head for Nolita and SoHo, where small (and often expensive) boutiques line the streets. Major franchises can also be found here, along Broadway, and side streets such as Prince Street, Broome Street and Spring Street. If you're planning a night out on the town, try the stores along Eighth Street that are popular among young clubbers, starting on Broadway and heading west.

Music

Although the growth of download has seen the demise of many of the large music retailers,

WINDOW SHOPPING

Start on Lexington between 59th and 60th streets: you'll see the flags outside Bloomingdale's. Walk west to Madison Avenue; between 60th and 61st streets is Barney's, for expensive clothing, jewelry, accessories and beauty products. Walk west along 57th Street, past Chanel and Christian Dior, to Henri Bendel and Bergdorf Goodman. On Fifth Avenue peer in at Gucci, Tiffany's and Prada.

Clockwise from top: Shirt store in SoHo; Colony Music on Broadway; a T-shirt that says it all; pretzels to go;

there is still much to delight the enthusiast. Branches of Academy Records boast collections of vintage classical and rock vinyl and used CDs; Colony Music at 1619 Broadway is the original "if you can't find it here, give up"; or check out the Metropolitan Opera Shop (www.metoperashop.org) for something more classical. Note: DVDs cannot be played on European machines.

Bargains

If you're looking for a bargain, try the popular sample sales, where designer brands are marked down as much as 80 percent. Designer sales are often held at open showrooms over a few days. Arrive early on the first day of the sale for the best selection, though prices do drop as days go by. To find out about upcoming sample sales pick up *New York* magazine or *Time Out New York*, or log onto www.dailycandy.com. For electronic goods try J and R Music & Computer (23 Park Row, tel 212/238-9000), plus other locations.

A Bite to Eat

As for food, in addition to the many upscale restaurants and cafés, simple NYC classics like hot dogs, pizza, bagels and frozen yogurt can be found on nearly every street corner, along with food carts selling anything from hot soft pretzels or candied almonds to six kinds of curry or falafel sandwiches—great street food.

FLEA MARKETS

You can find everything from silver and beaded jewelry to clothing, artworks and antiques at the weekend Annex Antique Fair & Flea Market (⊠ 125 W 18th Street, near Sixth Avenue ⏰ Dawn–dusk ⑂ $1). Uptown, check out the huge GreenFlea market on Sunday (⊠ Columbus Avenue between 76th and 77th streets ⏰ 10–6). There is a Saturday GreenFlea market in the Village (⊠ Greenwich Avenue and Charles Street ⏰ 11–7).

visit a weekend flea market; don't miss the Midtown department stores; a boutique in Greenwich Village

Directory

Lower Manhattan

Art
William Bennett Gallery
Books
The Mysterious Bookshop
Clothes
Abercrombie & Fitch
Resurrection
Discount
Century 21
Food and Wine
Kam Man Foods
Homewares
Pearl River Mart (▷ panel, 122)
Shoes
Alife Rivington Club
Brooks Brothers
Stationery
Kate's Paperie

Downtown and Chelsea

Accessories
Village Tannery
Clothes
Cynthia Rowley
Hotoveli
Jeffrey New York
Marc Jacobs
Scoop
Discount
DSW and Filene's
Loehmann's
Food and Wine
Chelsea Market
Union Square Greenmarket
Homewares
ABC Carpet and Home
Shoes
DSW and Filene's

Midtown

Department Stores
Bergdorf Goodman
Macy's
Saks Fifth Avenue

Homewares
Michael C. Fina
Shoes
Manolo Blahnik
Sports Goods
Nike Town NY
Technology
Apple Store
Toys
FAO Schwarz

Upper East Side and Central Park

Beauty
Zitomer
Books
Kitchen Arts and Letters
Clothes
Calvin Klein
Donna Karan
Ralph Lauren
Shanghai Tang
Department Stores
Barneys
Bloomingdale's

Upper West Side

Accessories
Laila Rowe
Beauty
Bluemercury Apothecary & Spa
Books
Barnes and Noble
Clothes
Betsey Johnson
Malia Mills
Steven Alan
Food and Wine
Zabar's
Shoes
Kenneth Cole
Sports Goods
Patagonia

SHOP

Shopping A–Z

ABC CARPET AND HOME
www.abchome.com
Here are seven floors of meticulously edited homewares, from four-poster beds to handkerchiefs, which share an esthetic that mixes Victorian brothel, mid-19th-century design museum, Venetian palace and deluxe hotel.

E15 ✉ 888 Broadway/E 19th Street ☎ 212/473-3000 🚇 4, 5, 6, N, Q, R 14th Street-Union Square

ABERCROMBIE & FITCH
www.abercrombie.com
Teens and college grads are the core customers at this temple to slouchy American style, famous for its rather racy Bruce Weber-shot catalogs. The clothes, though, are good for anyone's weekends and the prices are gentle. There are men's and women's lines.

F21 ✉ 199 Water Street/Fulton Street ☎ 212/809-9000 🚇 2, 3, 4, 5, A, C, J, Z Fulton Street-Broadway-Nassau

ALIFE RIVINGTON CLUB
Here, behind an unmarked door, sneakers are high fashion, with all the latest footwear from American, European and Japanese lines. Great colors and limited editions are available.

G18 ✉ 158 Rivington Street, between Clinton and Suffolk streets ☎ 212/375-8128 🚇 F, J, Z Delancey Street-Essex Street

APPLE STORE
www.apple.com
This 24-hour-a-day, 365-day-a-year showcase store is certain to delight ingrained Mac-geeks as well as the many trendy young things who fall under the spell of Apple's industry-leading design and stylish simplicity.

D9 ✉ 767 5th Avenue/59th Street ☎ 212/336-1440 🚇 N, R 5th Avenue-59th Street

BARNES AND NOBLE
www.barnesandnoble.com
This is one of the megabook chain's main New York branches. Check the website for upcoming evening readings.

B5 ✉ 2289 Broadway/82nd Street ☎ 212/362-8835, and branches 🚇 1 79th Street

The iconic 24-hour Apple Store on Fifth Avenue

A New York institution

BARNEYS

www.barneys.com

Many are the New Yorkers who dress exclusively from the *ne plus ultra* of high-fashion stores. Ranging over several floors are avant-garde designers, the store's own-label clothes, the city's best high-end cosmetics and scent departments, a huge range of hip jeans labels, great menswear, an epic shoe department, jewelry, homewares, kids' clothes and more. The prices are high.

🚇 E9 ✉ 660 Madison Avenue/61st Street ☎ 212/826-8900 🚈 N, R 5th Avenue-59th Street

BERGDORF GOODMAN

www.bergdorfgoodman.com

For the most sophisticated shopping experience in New York, the eight-floor fashion-for-lunching-ladies department store in the former Vanderbilt mansion takes the cake.

🚇 E9 ✉ 754 5th Avenue/58th Street ☎ 800/558-1855 🚈 N, R 5th Avenue-59th Street

BETSEY JOHNSON

www.betseyjohnson.com

This long-lived fashion darling produces fun looks for young women.

🚇 C7 ✉ 248 Columbus Avenue/71st Street ☎ 212/362-3364 🚈 1, 2, 3, B, C 72nd Street

BLOOMINGDALE'S

www.bloomingdales.com

Bloomingdale's opened in 1879 and is one of the most venerable names in Manhattan, yet it keeps up with the latest trends. The jewelry and handbag sections are particularly good.

🚇 F9 ✉ Lexington/59th Street ☎ 212/705-2000 🚈 4, 5, 6, F, N, R 59th Street

BLUEMERCURY APOTHECARY & SPA

www.bluemercury.com

From top brand cosmetics to spa treatments, hair care, famous fragrances and gorgeous candles, Bluemercury is a welcome addition to the Upper West Side retail experience.

🚇 B5 ✉ 2305 Broadway/83rd Street ☎ 212/799-0500 🚈 1 to 86th Street

THE SHOPS AT COLUMBUS CIRCLE

The closest thing to a mall in Manhattan, The Shops at Columbus Circle in the Time Warner Center has reclaimed Columbus Circle from the traffic. The stores are on the lowest four levels (restaurants above). The *pièce de résistance* is the Whole Foods Market.

🚇 C9 ✉ Time Warner Center, Broadway (59th/60th Street) ☎ 212/823-6300; www.shopsatcolumbuscircle.com 🚈 A, B, C, D, 1 59th Street-Columbus Circle

BROOKS BROTHERS

www.brooksbrothers.com

Home of the preppy, Brooks Brothers also caters to anyone, male or female (though the men's department is far better) who wants to look pulled together. Their basics, like boxer shorts and white dress shirts, are exceptional.

✚ E21 ✉ 1 Church Street/Liberty Plaza ☎ 212/267-2400 🚇 4, 5 Fulton Street

CALVIN KLEIN

www.calvinklein.com

The iconic New York designer's flagship store, designed by David Chipperfield, is as minimal as his clothing, without even racks to spoil the clean lines (you simply point at a display and request your size). His home line is downstairs.

✚ E9 ✉ 654 Madison Avenue/60th Street ☎ 212/292-9000 🚇 N, R 5th Avenue-59th Street

CENTURY 21

www.c21stores.com

Practically a cult, Century 21 sells discounted chic womenswear, especially by European designers.

✚ E21 ✉ 22 Cortlandt Street between Church Street and Broadway ☎ 212/227-9092 🚇 4, 5 Fulton Street

CHELSEA MARKET

www.chelseamarket.com

More than a store, this enormous city-block-size building is several villages' worth of food boutiques, bakeries, cafés, coffee shops and delis under one roof. Even if you're not hungry, it's enjoyable to stroll through for the architect-honed warehouse and inhale the mouth-watering aromas.

✚ C15 ✉ 75 9th Avenue/15th Street ☎ 212/243-6005 🚇 A, C, E, L 14th Street

CYNTHIA ROWLEY

www.cynthiarowley.com

Shop here to equip yourself for a night out on the town in adorable, hip dresses and shoes.

✚ C16 ✉ 376 Bleecker Street (between Perry and Charles streets) ☎ 212/242-3803 🚇 1 Christopher Street-Sheridan Square

DONNA KARAN

www.donnakaran.com

This beautiful bilevel space carries the home line, accessories and the best of new season Karan, as well as her lower-price lines.

✚ E8 ✉ 819 Madison Avenue/E 68th Street ☎ 212/861-1001 🚇 6 68th Street-Hunter College

DSW AND FILENE'S

www.dsw.com

www.filenesbasement.com

DSW stands for "Designer Shoe Warehouse". with Prada, Kate Spade, Via Spiga and others represented. Upstairs is a three-story Filene's where Dolce & Gabanna, Stella McCartney and Alberta Feretti are among the labels, with off-price off-season items on sale.

✚ E15 ✉ 4 Union Square South (University Place) ☎ 212/674-2146 🚇 L, N, Q, R, 4, 5, 6 Union Square

FAO SCHWARZ

www.fao.com

The near-legendary toy store has lost its iconic clockwork tower but gained a whole new lease of life. There are plenty of areas for kids to experiment with giant toys you have no intention of dragging home. Don't forget to dance on the piano from *Big*.

✚ E9 ✉ 767 5th Avenue/58th Street ☎ 212/644-9400 🚇 N, R 5th Avenue-59th Street

HOTOVELI

www.hotoveli.com

Chic French and Italian creations dominate in this West Village emporium, which caters for the style-conscious ladies and men about town.

🚩 C16 ✉ 271 W 4th Street, between Perry and W 11th streets ☎ 212/206-7722 🚇 1 Christopher Street-Sheridan Square

JEFFREY NEW YORK

www.jeffreynewyork.com

The coolest thing in the Meatpacking District, this compact department store of fashion for men and women is so high it has vertigo. A resident DJ, a spacious all-white interior and non-pushy assistants make for a pleasant visit—and an expensive one if you fall for the wares.

🚩 B15 ✉ 449 W 14th Street/Washington Street ☎ 212/206-3928 🚇 A, C, E, L 14th Street

KAM MAN FOODS

This large Chinese food store over-flows with exotic products, from live fish and edible birds' nests to ginseng priced at hundreds of dol-lars. It also sells Asian cookware.

🚩 F19 ✉ 200 Canal Street/Mott Street ☎ 212/571-0330 🚇 J, Z Canal Street

KATE'S PAPERIE

www.katespaperie.com

The handmade stationery is over-whelming at this SoHo boutique.

🚩 E18 ✉ 435 Broome Street, between Broadway and Crosby Street ☎ 212/941-9816 🚇 6 Spring Street

KENNETH COLE

www.kennethcole.com

Come here for quality shoes ranging from urban footwear to trendy fashion styles, and simple but stylish clothes for women and men, plus handbags, jewelry, sun-glasses and other accessories.

🚩 E11 ✉ 107 E 42nd Street/Park Avenue ☎ 212/949-8079 🚇 4, 5, 6, 7 Grand Central-42nd Street

KITCHEN ARTS AND LETTERS

www.kitchenartsandletters.com

This is a treasure trove of cook-books by leading authors including James Beard and Julia Child. You will find many rare and out-of-print titles as well as the very latest cookbook releases.

🚩 E4 ✉ 1435 Lexington Avenue, between 93rd and 94th streets ☎ 212/876-5550 🚇 6 96th Street

LAILA ROWE

www.lailarowe.com

This is one of a growing chain-ette of accessories stores, crammed with colorful gear. Expect a fun vibe and fast-changing selections of jewelry at prices that belie their on-the-money directional style.

🚩 C7 ✉ 253 Columbus Avenue/72nd Street ☎ 212/579-5254 🚇 B, C, 1, 2, 3 72nd Street

PEARL RIVER MART

Shop here for chrome lunch pails with clip-on lids; embroidered silk pajamas and Suzy Wong dresses; bamboo fans and porcelain rice bowls—all the things, in fact, you can get in the smaller Chinatown emporia, but collected under one roof. The food department sells an eclectic range. Prices are very, very low. 🚩 E18 ✉ 477 Broadway (Broome Street) ☎ 212/431-4770; www.pearlriver.com 🚇 N, R Canal Street

LOEHMANN'S

www.loehmanns.com

This store specializes in top designer labels at hugely reduced prices. Check out the Back Room on the fifth floor. There's another branch on the Upper West Side (Broadway at 73rd Street).

D15 ✉ 101 7th Avenue/17th Street ☎ 212/352-0856 🚇 1 18th Street

MACY'S

www.macys.com

The sign outside says it's the largest store in the world, and by the time you've made your way across the nine-block-long floors of this grandfather of all department stores, you'll believe it. You'll find everything here.

D12 ✉ 151 W 34th Street/Herald Square ☎ 212/695-4400 🚇 B, D, F, N, R 34th Street

MALIA MILLS

www.maliamills.com

This boutique swimwear emporium is cherished by every woman who fears her reflection: there are mix-and-match pieces made to fit everyone, in super-cool designs.

C7 ✉ 220 Columbus Avenue/70th Street ☎ 212/874-7200 🚇 1, 2, 3, B, C 72nd Street

MANOLO BLAHNIK

www.manoloblahnik.com

Fashionistas and celebrities alike come here for beautifully made shoes for by one of the world's great shoe designers.

D10 ✉ 31 W 54th Street ☎ 212/582-3007 🚇 E, M 5th Avenue-53rd Street

MARC JACOBS

www.marcjacobs.com

Fashion's favorite darling, Marc Jacobs put once-Bohemian Bleecker Street on the retail map.

C16 ✉ 403–405 Bleecker Street ☎ 212/924-0026 🚇 1, 2 Christopher Street-Sheridan Square

MICHAEL C. FINA

www.michaelcfina.com

This very exclusive purveyor of gifts and tableware is *the* place for wedding lists.

E11 ✉ 545 5th Avenue/45th Street ☎ 800/289-3462 🚇 4, 5, 6, 7 Grand Central

SHOP

The largest store in the world

THE MYSTERIOUS BOOKSHOP

www.mysteriousbookshop.com

This is a must for mystery lovers. Staff will lead you to new discoveries alongside writers such as Patricia Highsmith and Raymond Chandler. Rare books are available.

⊞ E20 ✉ 58 Warren Street/Church Street ☎ 212/587-1011 🚇 1, 2, 3, A, C, E Chambers Street

NIKE TOWN NY

www.nike.com

You can feel like a professional athlete here. High-tech videos and multilevel displays and an industrial atmosphere encourage aerobic shopping.

⊞ D9 ✉ 6 E 57th Street, between 5th and Madison avenues ☎ 212/891-6453 🚇 N, R 57th Street

PATAGONIA

www.patagonia.com

If you like environmental consciousness with your outdoor wear but still want to look slick while climbing the mountain, or just look like you might have done so, this is your place.

⊞ C6 ✉ 426 Columbus Avenue/81st Street ☎ 917/441-0011 🚇 B, C 81st Street-Museum of Natural History

RALPH LAUREN

www.ralphlauren.com

Distinguished cowboy and English country heritage looks are displayed in the Rhinelander Mansion, a turn-of-the-20th-century house.

⊞ E7 ✉ 867 Madison Avenue, between E 71st and 72nd streets ☎ 212/606-2100 🚇 6 68th Street-Hunter College

RESURRECTION

www.resurrectionvintage.com

You'll find a haul of pricey but perfect vintage, with an emphasis on collectable labels: Pucci, Halston, Courrèges, Dior. The owners offer their own line of skirts and tops.

⊞ F18 ✉ 217 Mott Street, between Spring and Prince streets ☎ 212/625-1374 🚇 6 Spring Street

SAKS FIFTH AVENUE

www.saksfifthavenue.com

This is the flagship store of the now nationwide chain, with a

For great designer vintage head for Resurrection on Mott Street

fabulous range of designer fashions for men and women.
🚇 E10 ✉ 611 5th Avenue/49th–50th streets ☎ 212/753-4000 🚊 E, F 5th Avenue

SCOOP

www.scoopnyc.com

This place has hip labels from Daryl K to Tocca and Katayone Adeli, plus cult items like James Perse T's.
🚇 B15 ✉ 430 W 14th Street/Washington Street ☎ 212/691-1905 🚊 A, C, E 14th Street

SHANGHAI TANG

www.shanghaitang.com

As the name suggests, this store sells youthful Asian-style clothing.
🚇 E8 ✉ 600 Madison Avenue ☎ 212/888-0111 🚊 F Lexington Avenue-63rd Street

STEVEN ALAN

www.stevenalan.com

A Lower East Side look on the Upper West Side, this is a carefully edited array of cutting-edge labels, some of them available nowhere else—including Alan's own designs.
🚇 B5 ✉ 465 Amsterdam Avenue/82nd Street ☎ 212/595-8451 🚊 1, 2, 3, 79th Street-Broadway; A, C, E 81st Street-Central Park West

VILLAGE TANNERY

www.villagetannery.com

Stylish handbags, designed by leather artisan Sevestet and hand-crafted from the finest materials, are made to order. The range extends to briefcases, backpacks, carry ons, belts and iPad covers.
🚇 D17 ✉ 173 Bleecker Street ☎ 212/673-5444 🚊 A, C, E, B, D, F, M West 4th Street-Washington Square

WILLIAM BENNETT GALLERY

www.williambennettgallery.com

Original works and rare prints by Picasso, Dalí, Warhol and Miró are displayed at this renowned gallery in the heart of SoHo's art district. It's fun to browse even if your budget doesn't stretch to buy.
🚇 E18 ✉ 65 Greene Street ☎ 212/965-8707 🚊 N, R Prince Street; 6, C, E Spring Street

ZABAR'S

www.zabars.com

The wise-cracking New Yawker of the foodie havens has a Jewish soul all its own. Cheese, coffee, smoked fish and the like are downstairs, while upstairs are the city's best buys in kitchenwares.
🚇 B6 ✉ 2245 Broadway/80th Street ☎ 212/787-2000 🚊 1 79th Street

ZITOMER

www.zitomer.com

At root, an über-drugstore, this Upper East Side classic encompasses everything from toys to pet accessories. The number of bath, body and skincare ranges is impressive and it's the best place to shop for hair accessories.
🚇 E6 ✉ 969 Madison Avenue/76th Street ☎ 212/737-5560 🚊 6 77th Street

Entertainment

Once you've done with sightseeing for the day, you'll find lots of other great things to do with your time in this chapter, even if all you want to do is relax with a drink. In this section establishments are listed alphabetically.

ENTERTAINMENT

Introduction

As the sun sets over New York, the city becomes a sultry, romantic and mysterious place. For spectacular sunset views stroll along the pedestrian path on the banks of the Hudson River on the West Side, then wander through Times Square as the electric billboards pop out from the dark sky.

Nightlife

As young New Yorkers explore new frontiers in the city, the Meatpacking District—once known for drugs and prostitution—has become home to trendy bars and clubs. Celebrity sightings are common at Spice Market (403 W 13th Street, tel 212/675-2322) and 5 Ninth (5 9th Avenue, tel 212/929-9460). At the other end of the spectrum are biker bars like Hogs & Heifers Saloon (859 Washington Street at W 13th Street, tel 212/929-0655) and Fat Cat Billiards (75 Christopher Street in West Village, tel 212/675-6056), friendly dives where the beer flows cheaply and the music is loud.

A short stroll away, a string of music bars sit cheek by jowl along two blocks of Bleecker Street between La Guardia Place and Sullivan Street, including the venerable folk-rock haven, The Bitter End (147 Bleecker Street, tel 212/673-7030), still going strong after more than 50 years. Around the corner is Café Wha? (▷ 133), where Dylan and Hendrix once played, now a dance club.

FOR A LAUGH

Comedy clubs are a great way to sample New York's sense of humor. Venues such as Caroline's (✉ 1626 Broadway, at 50th Street ☎ 212/757-4100; www.carolines.com), Upright Citizens Brigade Theatre (✉ 307 W 26th Street, between 8th and 9th ☎ 212/366-9176; www.ucbtheatre. com), Stand Up NY (▷ 137) and Gotham (▷ 134) are popular. The Laurie Beechman Theatre (▷ 134) hosts regular performances by the legendary Joan Rivers.

Clockwise from top: Blue Note in Greenwich Village is one of the best places for jazz; the old Paramount Theater, Times Square; Alice Tully Hall, the Lincoln

Another hot nightlife neighborhood is the Lower East Side, where there's a raft of rock 'n' roll bars fanning out from Ludlow and Stanton streets. Leading the pack are Arlene's Grocery (▷ 131), Pianos (158 Ludlow Street, tel 212/505-3733) and Cake Shop (152 Ludlow Street, tel 212/253-0036).

Broadway and Beyond

Top Broadway shows can be expensive, but you can pick up some great bargains at the TKTS booth in Times Square and other locations (www.tdf.org/tkts). Off-Broadway venues are less expensive and you might just catch the next big hit on its way up. A night at Lincoln Center (▷ 42–43) is an unforgettable New York experience, whether you opt for a production at the Metropolitan Opera (▷ 135), a symphony at Avery Fisher Hall (▷ 131), a ballet at the David H. Koch Theater, or one of the more intimate venues.

Take to the Water

Circle Line Cruises' evening boat rides around Manhattan are a relaxing and memorable way to experience the world's most famous skyline. Board at Pier 83, at 42nd Street on the Hudson River (tel 212/563-3200). Tour guides on board relate the legends of the city (www.circleline42.com).

LIVE MUSIC

Rock bands perform at Bowery Ballroom (✉ 6 Delancey Street; www.boweryballroom.com) and The Fillmore New York @ Irving Plaza (✉ 17 Irving Plaza; www.irvingplaza.com), while Madison Square Garden (▷ 135) hosts blockbuster tours. You can hear everything from classical music to pop at Carnegie Hall (▷ 133). Among the top jazz clubs are Blue Note (▷ 132) in Greenwich Village, Iridium (✉ 1650 Broadway; www.iridiumjazzclub.com) and Village Vanguard (✉ 178 7th Avenue South; www.villagevanguard.com).

Center; Gotham Comedy Club; a quiet table à deux in the Meatpacking District; an evening cruise is a great way to see the New York skyline by night

Directory

Lower Manhattan

Bars
Barramundi
Bridge Café
Parkside Lounge
The Porterhouse at Fraunces
   Tavern
Clubs
Arlene's Grocery
Beach at Governors Island
S.O.B.'s
Comedy
Comedy Cellar

Downtown and Chelsea

Bars
McSorley's Old Ale House
Pete's Tavern
Vintage Irving
White Horse Tavern
Cabaret/Burlesque
Duplex (▷ panel, 134)
Joe's Pub
Lips (▷ panel, 134)
Clubs
Café Wha?
Comedy
Gotham Comedy Club
Jazz
Blue Note
Karaoke
Sing Sing Karaoke
Live Music
Mercury Lounge
Theater/Performance
PS 122

Midtown

Bars
Empire Hotel Rooftop Bar
Four Seasons Hotel
Classical Music
Carnegie Hall
Comedy
The Laurie Beechman Theatre
Jazz
Birdland

Live Music
Best Buy Theater
Madison Square Garden
Theater/Performance
The New Victory Theater
New World Stages
Radio City Music Hall
TV Show Recording
The Late Show with David
   Letterman

Upper East Side and Central Park

Bars
Auction House
Roof Garden Café and Martini Bar
   at the Met
Stone Rose Lounge
Cabaret
Feinsteins at Loews Regency
Comedy
Dangerfield's
Jazz
Café Carlyle
Café Pierre
Literary Events/Readings
92nd Street Y
Theater/Performance
Florence Gould Hall

Upper West Side

Cinema
Lincoln Plaza Cinema
Classical Music
Avery Fisher Hall
Bruno Walter Auditorium
Cathedral of St. John the Divine
The Metropolitan Opera
New York City Opera
Comedy
Stand Up NY
Jazz
Dizzy's Club Coca Cola
Smoke
Theater/Performance
Beacon Theatre
Symphony Space

Entertainment A–Z

92ND STREET Y
www.92Y.org
A varied program of events includes readings by renowned authors, folk, jazz and lectures that cover a wide range of subjects.
➕ E4 ✉ Kauffman Concert Hall, 1395 Lexington Avenue/92nd Street ☎ 212/415-5500 🚇 6 96th Street

ARLENE'S GROCERY
www.arlenesgrocery.net
This is one of the best rock clubs in the city, where hot new bands make their name.
➕ G18 ✉ 95 Stanton Street, between Ludlow and Orchard streets ☎ 212/995-1652 🚇 F, M 2nd Avenue

AUCTION HOUSE
With red velvet drapes, a fireplace, sofas and candlelight, this is more suited to a romantic drink than a rowdy night out. The no-furs, no-sneakers dress code gives an idea of the casual-chic ambience.
➕ F4 ✉ 300 E 89th Street/Second Avenue ☎ 212/427-4458 🚇 4, 5, 6 86th Street

AVERY FISHER HALL
www.new.lincolncenter.org
The home of the New York Philharmonic, the Avery Fisher Hall seats 2,700. It is also home to other organizations including the American Symphony Orchestra.
➕ B8 ✉ 10 Lincoln Center Plaza, Columbus Avenue/65th Street ☎ 212/875-5030 🚇 1 66th Street-Lincoln Center

Check out the cocktails

BARRAMUNDI
www.barramundiny.com
Woodsy decor, a neighborhood crowd, Aussie beers and a new flavor of infused vodka every week are among the draws at this Lower East Side hangout.
➕ G18 ✉ 67 Clinton Street near Rivington Street ☎ 212/529-6999 🚇 F, J, Z Delancey Street-Essex Street

BEACH AT GOVERNORS ISLAND
www.thebeachconcerts.com
This outdoor venue for live events with bars, café and beer garden has views of the Manhattan skyline as you boogie to DJs and big-name bands.
➕ Off map ✉ Governors Island ☎ No phone 🚢 Water Taxi from Battery Maritime Building Slip at 10 South Street

ENTERTAINMENT

COCKTAIL CULTURE

Cocktail culture is alive and well in the Big Apple. The Martini craze is here to stay—many lounges and bars offer long menus of creative concoctions. Elegant glassware is crucial. Atmospheres range from urban chic to clubby lounge to pubs. Neighborhood pubs, with more emphasis on beer and bourbon, are favorite watering holes. Or, instead of alcohol, visit one of New York's coffee bars.

Carnegie Hall

Village jazz club and restaurant.
⊞ D17 ✉ 131 W 3rd Street/6th Avenue–MacDougal Street ☎ 212/475-8592 🚇 A, C, E, B, D, F 4th Street-Washington Square

BRIDGE CAFÉ
www.bridgecafenyc.com
This loveable place has been serving continuously since 1794—yes, it's one of the oldest taverns in town. The bar is a lovely place to end an evening after a stroll by the East River.
⊞ F21 ✉ 279 Water Street/Dover Street ☎ 212/227-3344 🚇 4, 5, 6 Brooklyn Bridge-City Hall

BRUNO WALTER AUDITORIUM
www.lincolncenter.org
Come here for a wide range of seminars, lectures, films, recitals and concerts.
⊞ B8 ✉ The New York Library for the Performing Arts, 111 Amsterdam Avenue between 64th and 65th streets ☎ 212/870-1630 🚇 1 66th Street-Lincoln Center

CAFÉ CARLYLE
www.thecarlyle.com
This lounge in the elegant Carlyle Hotel was home to the great Bobby Short until his death in 2005, but his spirit lives on in the piano player, lounge singers and jazz bands. Be sure to look in at Bemelman's Bar.
⊞ E6 ✉ Carlyle Hotel, Madison Avenue/76th Street ☎ 212/744-1600 🚇 6 77th Street

CAFÉ PIERRE
You can relax over jazz and cabaret songs, plus requests, from Nancy Winston and Kathleen Landis.
⊞ E9 ✉ Pierre Hotel, 2 E 61st Street/5th Avenue ☎ 212/838-8000 🚇 N, R 5th Avenue-59th Street

BEACON THEATRE
www.beacontheatre.com
Beacon offers storytelling, readings, children's performance, music, dance and much more.
⊞ B7 ✉ 2124 Broadway/74th Street ☎ 212/465-6500 🚇 1, 2, 3 72nd Street

BEST BUY THEATER
www.bestbuytheater.com
This is a medium-size venue for medium-big acts in the center of Times Square.
⊞ C11/D11 ✉ 1515 Broadway/44th Street ☎ 212/930-1959 🚇 1, 2, 3, 7, N, Q, R, S Times Square-42nd Street

BIRDLAND
www.birdlandjazz.com
Big names, big bands, John Coltrane tributes and Cubans are the range here.
⊞ C11 ✉ 315 W 44th Street/8th–9th avenues ☎ 212/581-3080 🚇 A, C, E 42nd Street-Port Authority Bus Terminal

BLUE NOTE
www.bluenote.net
Jazz artists from around the world play two shows nightly at this

CAFÉ WHA?

www.cafewha.com

In business since the 1950s, this has been a hot spot ever since Bob Dylan and Jimi Hendrix used to hang out here. The Boss started his career here. It's still going strong with bands performing nightly and styles ranging from R&B, funk and jazz to soul and modern rock.

D17 ✉ 115 MacDougal/Bleecker-W 3rd Street ☎ 212/254-3706 🚇 A, B, C, D, E, F, M 4th Street-Washington Square

CARNEGIE HALL

www.carnegiehall.org

This world-class recital hall features an eclectic program from classical artists to folk singers, world music and pop.

D9 ✉ 881 7th Avenue/57th Street ☎ 212/247-7800 🚇 N, R 57th Street; E 7th Avenue

CATHEDRAL OF ST. JOHN THE DIVINE

www.stjohndivine.org

The cathedral provides a varied program of liturgical, cultural and civic events.

B1 ✉ 1047 Amsterdam Avenue/112th Street ☎ 212/ 316-7490 🚇 1 Cathedral Parkway-110th Street

COMEDY CELLAR

www.comedycellar.com

A cozy Greenwich Village spot, this attracts well-known comedians from time to time. The intimate nature of the venue means you are quite likely to find you are part of the show.

17 ✉ 117 Macdougal Street, between W 3rd Street and Minetta Lane ☎ 212/254-3480 🚇 A, B, C, D, E, F, M 4th Street-Washington Square

DANGERFIELD'S

www.dangerfields.com

This club, established in 1969, is still going strong. Those who have performed here include Jay Leno and Jim Carrey.

F9 ✉ 1118 1st Avenue/61st Street ☎ 212/593-1650 🚇 4, 5, 6 59th Street

DIZZY'S CLUB COCA COLA

www.jalc.org/dccc

Jazz at Lincoln Center's intimate club is—in the spirit of Dizzy Gillespie—designed to ensure that performers and spectators alike relaaaaax. There are also After Hours sets Tuesday through Saturday nights.

C9 ✉ Time Warner Center at Broadway/60th Street, 5th floor ☎ 212/258-9800 🚇 A, B, C, D, 1 59th Street-Columbus Circle

EMPIRE HOTEL ROOFTOP BAR

www.empirehotelnyc.com

There are fabulous views over Lincoln Center from the 12th-floor deck of this luxury hotel—and a chic atmosphere with candlelit tables, banquettes and greenery.

C8 ✉ 44 W 63rd Street/Broadway ☎ 212/265-7400 🚇 1 66th Street-Lincoln Center

KEEPING UP

One of New York's favorite pastimes is keeping up with what's on. Look for extensive weekly listings in the magazines *New York*, *Time Out New York* and *New Yorker*, or the Friday and Sunday editions of the *New York Times*. You can also pick up free copies of the *Village Voice* and *New York Press* newspapers in storefronts and vestibules around town. The monthly listings in *Paper* magazine have a decidedly Downtown focus.

FEINSTEINS AT LOEWS REGENCY

www.feinsteinsattheregency.com

The cabaret star Michael Feinstein performs at his namesake venue only a couple of times a year but the rest of the time he manages to secure top Broadway names for this swanky, intimate room.

⊞ E9 ⊠ Regency Hotel, 540 Park Avenue/61st Street ☎ 212/339-4095 🚇 N, R Lexington Avenue-59th Street

FLORENCE GOULD HALL

The 400-seat venue is associated with the Alliance Française. Events include opera, pop singers, dance, jazz and readings.

⊞ E9 ⊠ 55 E 59th Street/Park–Madison avenues ☎ 212/355-6100 🚇 N, R 5th Avenue-59th Street

FOUR SEASONS HOTEL

www.fourseasons.com

I. M. Pei design, a sleek energy and a great Martini menu make this a great choice for cocktails.

⊞ E9 ⊠ 57 E 57th Street/ Madison Avenue ☎ 212/758-5700 🚇 4, 5, 6 Lexington Avenue-59th Street

GOTHAM COMEDY CLUB

www.gothamcomedyclub.com

Gotham showcases top stars as well as up-and-coming comedians.

⊞ C14 ⊠ 208 W 23rd Street/7th Avenue ☎ 212/367-9000 🚇 N, R, 1 23rd Street; F, Path 23rd Street

JOE'S PUB

www.joespub.com

The red velvet bar and performance space always has an interesting line-up of singers, comedians, magicians and burlesque artistes.

⊞ E16 ⊠ The Public Theater, 425 Lafayette Street/Astor Place ☎ 212/967-7555 🚇 N, R 8th Street-NYU; 6 Astor Place

THE LATE SHOW WITH DAVID LETTERMAN

www.cbs.com

Catch the top-rated US chat show at one of its weeknight outings in the heart of theaterland. Letterman draws A-list names.

⊞ C10 ⊠ 1697 Broadway 🚇 1 50th Street-Broadway

THE LAURIE BEECHMAN THEATRE

www.beechmantheatre.com

This basement supper club hosts regular performances by comedy legend Joan Rivers.

⊞ B11 ⊠ 407 W 42nd Street/9th Avenue ☎ 212/695-6909 🚇 1, 2, 3, 7, N, Q, R Times Square-42nd Street

LINCOLN PLAZA CINEMA

www.lincolnplazacinema.com

Several screens show successful first runs and also foreign movies.

⊞ B8 ⊠ 1886 Broadway/63rd Street ☎ 212/757-2280 🚇 1 66th Street-Lincoln Center

---

CABARET

The term has undergone so many image overhauls, it's now settled into being a catch-all for entertainment options ranging from off-Broadway cabaret theater and downtown crooners sitting around the piano bar at Duplex (⊠ 61 Christopher Street ☎ 212/255-5438; www.theduplex.com) to drag queen lip-synching and, in the case of Lips (⊠ 227 E 56th Street ☎ 212/675-7710; www.lipsnyc.com), Bitchy Bingo. Joe's Pub (above) is among the venues that offer what you might call classic, though modernized, cabaret.

MADISON SQUARE GARDEN

www.thegarden.com

The giant concrete circle is one of the city's major venues for music and sporting events. For the box office enter the Main Ticket Lobby at 7th Avenue and 32nd Street.

➕ C13 ✉ 4 Pennsylvania Plaza 🚇 1, 2, 3 34th Street-Penn Station

MCSORLEY'S OLD ALE HOUSE

www.mcsorleysnewyork.com

New York's oldest saloon (1854) draws a crowd with its sawdust-covered floors, coal-burning stove and working-class history. Belly up to the mahogany bar for a pint of its golden ale.

➕ F16 ✉ 15 E 7th Street/3rd Avenue ☎ 212/474-9148 🚇 6 Astor Place

MERCURY LOUNGE

www.mercuryloungenyc.com

Its laid-back atmosphere attracts eclectic performers.

➕ F17 ✉ 217 E Houston Street/Avenue A ☎ 212/260-4700 🚇 F 2nd Avenue

THE METROPOLITAN OPERA

www.metoperafamily.org

The gala openings at this world-class opera rank among the most glamorous of the city's cultural events. Line up on Saturday mornings for inexpensive standing-room tickets. The season runs from October to April.

➕ B8 ✉ 30 Lincoln Center ☎ 212/362-6000 🚇 1 66th Street/Lincoln Center

THE NEW VICTORY THEATER

www.newvictory.org

If you have kids (over five) in tow, there'll be something here to thrill them. It offers one of the best youth-centric programs.

➕ C11 ✉ 209 W 42nd Street/7th–8th avenues ☎ 646/223-3010 🚇 1, 2, 3, 7, N, R, Q Times Square-42nd Street

NEW WORLD STAGES

www.newworldstages.com

Check out the top off-Broadway productions, from musicals to kids' shows, at this state-of-the-art theatrical venue.

➕ C10 ✉ 340 W 50th Street/8th Avenue ☎ 212/239-6200 🚇 C, E 50th Street

NEW YORK CITY OPERA

www.nycopera.com

The Met's neighbor offers new works, operetta and musicals.

➕ B8 ✉ David H. Koch Theater, 20 Lincoln Center ☎ 212/870-5570 🚇 1 66th Street-Lincoln Center

ENTERTAINMENT

PARKSIDE LOUNGE

www.parksidelounge.net

A multipurpose venue, Parkside hosts live music, stand-up and karaoke, and people just having a beer. It's open until 4am and is an unpretentious place to sample the Lower East Side buzz.

⊞ G17 ⊠ 317 E Houston Street/Attorney Avenue ☎ 212/673-6270 🚇 F, M 2nd Avenue

PETE'S TAVERN

www.petestavern.com

This 1864 Gramercy Park Victorian saloon is where O. Henry wrote *The Gift of the Magi*. No matter how hokey its history, it is a favorite, with a welcoming feel.

⊞ E15 ⊠ 129 E 18th Street/Irving Place ☎ 212/473-7676 🚇 L, N, R, 4, 6 14th Street-Union Square

Famous since the 1930s

THE PORTERHOUSE AT FRAUNCES TAVERN

www.frauncestavern.com

This 18th-century watering hole, where George Washington bade goodbye to his officers after the Revolutionary War, is the first stateside branch of Dublin's Porterhouse Brewing Company. It has fine ales, stouts, guest beers and an adjoining restaurant.

⊞ E22 ⊠ 54 Pearl Street ☎ 212/968-1776 🚇 N, R Whitehall Street

PS 122

www.ps122.org

A converted public school, PS 122 hosts unusual performance art, from bizarre to poignant.

⊞ F16 ⊠ 150 1st Avenue/E 9th Street ☎ 212/477-5829 🚇 N, R 8th Street; F 2nd Avenue

RADIO CITY MUSIC HALL

www.radiocity.com

This landmark art deco theater, which opened in 1932, hosts several music shows a year. You can also take an hour-long tour.

⊞ D10 ⊠ 1260 6th Avenue/50th Street ☎ 212/307-7171 🕐 Varied. Tours daily 11–3 🚇 B, D, F, M 40th–50th streets-Rockefeller Center

ROOF GARDEN CAFÉ AND MARTINI BAR AT THE MET

www.metmuseum.org

You can get cocktails and simple food on this rooftop terrace with bits of its sponsors' sculpture collection among the wisteria trellises and a heavenly view of Central Park treetops. Access is by elevators on the far southwest corner. It's open May through late fall (weather permitting).

⊞ D5 ✉ Metropolitan Museum of Art, 1000 5th Avenue/82nd Street ☎ 212/535-7710 🚇 6 86th Street

SING SING KARAOKE
www.karaokesingsing.com
Sing your heart out in this popular karaoke venue, which regularly updates its song list.

⊞ G17 ✉ 81 Avenue A/E 5th and 6th Street ☎ 212/674-0700 🚇 F, M Lower East Side-2nd Avenue

SMOKE
www.smokejazz.com
Plush couches adorn this intimate lounge, which hosts great jazz artists and local favorites.

⊞ B2 ✉ 2751 Broadway/105th Street ☎ 212/864-6662 🚇 1 103rd Street

S.O.B.'S
www.sobs.com
The Latin beat keeps you dancing at the tropically themed nightclub Sounds of Brazil. Hear African, reggae and other island music.

⊞ D18 ✉ 200 Varick Street ☎ 212/243-4940 🚇 1 Houston Street

STAND UP NY
www.standupny.com
This is a traditional comedy club where new and aspiring comics test their routines.

⊞ B6 ✉ 236 W 78th Street/ Broadway ☎ 212/595-0850 🚇 1 79th Street

STONE ROSE LOUNGE
Enjoy impressive design, fine food and drink, and stunning views of Central Park and Broadway.

⊞ C9 ✉ 10 Times Warner Center, Columbus Circle ☎ 212/823 9769 🚇 A, B, C, D 59th Street-Columbus Circle

SYMPHONY SPACE
www.symphonyspace.org
Storytelling, readings, children's theater, music, dance and more are on offer here.

⊞ B4 ✉ 2537 Broadway/95th Street ☎ 212/864-5400 🚇 1, 2, 3 96th Street

VINTAGE IRVING
www.vintageirving.com
Exposed brick and wood furniture give a European feel. Imbibe fine wines and cocktails and don't leave without trying a *pinot noir* flavored Wine Cellar Sorbet.

⊞ E15 ✉ 118 E 15th Street/Irving Place ☎ 212/677-6300 🚇 L 3rd Avenue

WHITE HORSE TAVERN
This sprawling 1880s bar was the last watering hole of Welsh poet Dylan Thomas, whose portrait still hangs in the middle room. There are sidewalk tables in summer.

⊞ C16 ✉ 567 Hudson Street/11th Street ☎ 212/989-3956 🚇 1 Christopher Street-Sheridan Square

BIG IN NEW YORK
From the elegance of a grand opera to the excitement of avant-garde performance art, New York spectacles are world-class (even the flops). Broadway shows can be expensive, but nothing transports audiences like a great multimillion-dollar musical or an intense performance by a drama diva. Be sure to reserve tickets in advance for the most popular shows.

Eat

There are places to eat across the city to suit all tastes and budgets. In this section establishments are listed alphabetically.

EAT

Introduction

From basic diners serving trademark large portions to über-trendy chefs and restaurants showcasing world cuisine, New York really can claim to offer something to suit every taste, diet and most budgets.

Around the World
In this global melting pot it's almost impossible not to find just about every cuisine in the world. Kosher, Polish, Italian, Greek and Chinese have pride of place but you will also find everything from Afghan to Russian. To get a flavor of the city's culinary heritage check out a food tour such as the one offered by New York Fun Tours (www.newyorkfuntours.com).

A Day's Dining
No one does "breakfast" or brunch like Manhattanites (especially at weekends) so make for Greenwich Village or SoHo, grab a copy of the *New York Times* and just chill over your choice of eggs, bacon, pancakes or waffles and limitless coffee. For lunch, try a Jewish deli for plenty of atmosphere and gargantuan sandwiches; make for the Food Court on the lower level of Grand Central Terminal (▷ 145); or, if you're downtown, Chinatown or Little Italy should help keep you fueled for the rest of the day's shopping or sightseeing. Dinner in New York can be as casual or as stylish as your mood and budget dictate.

TAXES, TIPPING AND FINANCIAL MATTERS

A sales tax of 8.875 percent will be added to your dining bill. The minimum tip (with good service) is 15 percent; people often double the tax for a 17.75 percent tip. Many restaurants offer fixed-price menus, which are good value. Watch for New York Restaurant Week in February, a special promotion offering a three-course menu at reduced rates for lunch and dinner at many restaurants; this promotion is often extended so it's always worth checking if it's available.

From top: Pancakes with maple syrup in a New York diner; the city has some great pizzerias; Café Boulud, a top restaurant; cheeseburger with fries

EAT

Directory

Lower Manhattan

Asian
Nobu
Casual
The Bailey Pub & Brasserie
Bubby's
Delicatessen
Schillers
Classic NY
Katz's Deli
Odeon (▷ panel, 142)
European
Double Crown
Italian
Travertine

Downtown and Chelsea

Asian
Almond
Yama (▷ panel, 144)
Contemporary
Gotham Bar and Grill
North Square
The Spotted Pig
Italian
Del Posto
Mexican
Mary Ann's
Polish/Ukrainian
Veselka

Midtown

Casual
Grand Central Terminal Food Court
   (▷ panel, 145)
John's
Classic NY
'21' Club
Four Seasons
Oyster Bar
Contemporary
Le Bernardin
Casa Lever
Per Se
European
Uncle Nick's

Upper East Side and Central Park

Casual
Jackson Hole
Serendipity 3
Contemporary
Café Boulud
Daniel
Classic NY
Loeb Boathouse
Oak Room
European
Café Sabarsky

Upper West Side

Asian
Fatty Crab
Casual
Barney Greengrass
Boat Basin Café
Contemporary
Jean-Georges
Ouest
Picholine
Tolani Wine Restaurant
Italian
Carmine's

Further Afield

Casual
Grimaldi's
Classic NY
Peter Luger
Contemporary
Blue Ribbon
Grocery
Henry's End
River Café
Sherwood Café (▷ panel, 148)

EAT

Eating A–Z

PRICES

Prices are approximate, based on a 3-course meal for one person.

$$$ over $60
$$ $40–$60
$ under $40

'21' CLUB $$$

www.21club.com

With a history spanning more than eight decades, this eatery nods a cap to its speakeasy days. Choose from fixed-price menus or an extensive à la carte featuring lobster, steak, salmon and much more. The '21' burger is a favorite.
➕ D10 ✉ 21 W 52nd Street/5th–6th avenues ☎ 212/582–7200 🕐 Mon–Sat lunch and dinner 🚇 B, D, F, M 47th–50th streets-Rockefeller Center

ALMOND $$

www.almondnyc.com

This buzzing American bistro uses the freshest ingredients from farm to table; reservations are essential. It's a warm friendly space often filled with a trendy crowd. The sea scallops are not to be missed and it seems a shame to have to share the apple cinnamon crisp for two.
➕ E14 ✉ 12 E 22nd Street/Broadway-Park Avenue ☎ 212/228-7557 🕐 Daily lunch and dinner, weekend brunch
🚇 R 23rd Street

THE BAILEY PUB & BRASSERIE $–$$

www.thebaileynyc.com

Just off Wall Street, this is a big hit with the Financial District crowd. The bar, which stays open until 1am, serves British pub-style food. The Brasserie offers excellent yet inexpensive meals, from salads and sandwiches through to steaks and a *plat du jour*.
➕ E22 ✉ 52 William Street ☎ 212/859-2200 🕐 Daily breakfast, lunch and dinner, weekend brunch 🚇 A, C Broadway-Nassau; 2, 3, 4, 5 Wall Street

BARNEY GREENGRASS $

www.barneygreengrass.com

An Upper West Side tradition since 1929, this is frantic on weekends, when locals feast on huge platters of smoked fish—whitefish, sable, sturgeon and lox—or sandwiches made with similar ingredients.
➕ B5 ✉ 541 Amsterdam Avenue/86th Street ☎ 212/724-4707 🕐 Tue–Sun 8–6 🚇 1 86th Street

LE BERNARDIN $$$

www.le-bernardin.com

Frenchman Eric Ripert is acknowledged to be the fish maestro. Exquisite, inventive dishes are served by super-attentive waiters.
➕ D10 ✉ 155 W 51st Street/7th Avenue ☎ 212/554-1515 🕐 Closed Sat lunch, Sun 🚇 B, D, F, M 47th–50th streets-Rockefeller Center

ODEON $$

After celebrating its quarter-century in 2005 with all the '80s faces that made it the first hot spot of the *Bright Lights, Big City* age, this art deco-style restaurant still outdoes half the new *boîtes* in town. Its tiled floors, dim lighting, happy bar area and open-most-hours welcome are some reasons why—that and the always-reliable nouvelle-American cooking.
➕ D20 ✉ 145 West Broadway/Thomas Street ☎ 212/233-0507; www.theodeonrestaurant.com 🕐 Daily lunch and dinner, Sat–Sun brunch and dinner 🚇 A, C Chambers Street

BLUE RIBBON $$

There's a Manhattan feel to this huge modern-American favorite in Brooklyn, and that's not surprising since it has an older sister there (97 Sullivan Street/Prince Street), liked by off-duty chefs. It combines creative and comfort food.

➕ Off map to southeast ✉ 280 5th Avenue/1st Street, Brooklyn ☎ 718/840-0404 🕐 Daily dinner 🚇 R Union Street

BOAT BASIN CAFÉ $

www.boatbasincafe.com

It's hard to find this unpretentious place serving diner-style food on the banks of the Hudson, but if you do it's worth waiting for a terrace table. The view is dazzling.

➕ A6 ✉ W 79th Street/Hudson River ☎ 212/496-5542 🕐 Late Mar–Oct (weather permitting) daily lunch and dinner 🚇 1 79th Street

BUBBY'S $

www.bubbys.com

A Tribeca favorite, Bubby's serves all-American BLTs, chicken clubs, meat loaf and fries, followed by pies (cherry, apple, chocolate peanut butter, etc). Expect a wait for the popular weekend brunch.

➕ D19 ✉ 120 Hudson Street ☎ 718/219-0666 🕐 Tue–Sun 24 hours, Mon till midnight 🚇 1, 9 Franklin Street; A, C, E Canal Street

CAFÉ BOULUD $$–$$$

www.cafeboulud.com

A favorite Daniel Boulud restaurant with classical, seasonal and ethnic influences. You will find *pot au feu*, *bouillabaisse* and entrées inspired by Spain, Morocco and Vietnam.

➕ E6 ✉ 20 E 76th Street/5th–Madison avenues ☎ 212/772-2600 🕐 Tue–Sun lunch and dinner, Mon dinner only, closed public holidays 🚇 6 77th Street

CAFÉ SABARSKY $–$$

www.cafesabarsky.com

The restaurant in the Neue Galerie has New York's premier Austrian chef, Kurt Gutenbrunner at the helm. You can also just drop in for coffee and cake.

➕ E5 ✉ Neue Galerie New York, 1048 5th Avenue/86th Street ☎ 212/288-0665 🕐 Mon and Wed 9–6, Thu–Sun 9–9, closed Tue 🚇 4, 5, 6 86th Street

EAT

Bubby's in Tribeca is a favorite choice for weekend brunch

CARMINE'S $$

www.carminesnyc.com

This beloved, raucous place serves Sicilian-Italian dishes family-style—huge platters to share. It's not for picky foodies, but it's fun.

⊞ B4 ⊠ 2450 Broadway/90th Street
☎ 212/362-2200 ⊙ Daily lunch and dinner ⊚ 1, 2, 3 96th Street/Broadway

CASA LEVER $$–$$$

www.casalever.com

The ocean liner-esque design is the star at this restaurant, downstairs in the 1952 Lever House building on Park Avenue, but it would be worth visiting for chef Bradford Thompson's contemporary menu alone. It features new twists on northern Italian classics.

⊞ E10 ⊠ 390 Park Avenue/53rd Street
☎ 212/888-2700 ⊙ Mon–Fri breakfast, lunch and dinner, Sat brunch and dinner, closed Sun ⊚ E, M Lexington Avenue-53rd Street; 6 51st Street

DANIEL $$$

www.danielnyc.com

This formal restaurant serves exquisitely restrained, modern French dishes—opt for the six-course tasting menu to appreciate fully chef Daniel Boulud's brilliance. Dessert arrives with its own basket of warm madeleines.

⊞ E8 ⊠ 60 E 65th Street/Madison–Park avenues ☎ 212/288-0033 ⊙ Mon–Sat dinner, closed Sun ⊚ 6 68th Street-Hunter College

DEL POSTO $$$

www.delposto.com

Mario Batali is New York's rotundly ebullient TV-friendly patron saint of interesting Italian food, known for rustic dishes and casual ambience. Here he has changed the rules: This is a swanky, deco-looking, big-night-out restaurant, with piano player, tableside preparations and valet parking. It works beautifully.

⊞ B15 ⊠ 85 10th Avenue/16th Street
☎ 212/497-8090 ⊙ Mon–Fri lunch and dinner, Sat–Sun dinner ⊚ A, C, E, L 14th Street

DELICATESSEN $

www.delicatessennyc.com

In need of some comfort food? Then head for this funky SoHo restaurant. Start with Grandma's meatloaf then polish off with milk and cookies.

⊞ D18 ⊠ 54 Prince Street ☎ 212/226-0211 ⊙ Daily lunch and dinner ⊚ N, R Prince Street

DOUBLE CROWN $–$$

www.doublecrown-nyc.com

The British Empire meets its former colonies in this original presentation of colonial food from South East Asia and India in a shabby-chic restaurant. Start with rice noodles and follow with bangers and mash.

⊞ F17 ⊠ 316 Bowery/Bleecker streets
☎ 212/254-0350 ⊙ Daily dinner, Sat–Sun brunch and dinner

GIANT SUSHI

For the sushi connoisseur, Yama ($) may not offer the best there is, but it does serve the biggest sushi and it is good. Sadly, many people share this view, and the tiny place is inundated with salivating sushi wolves, who line up to eat here.

⊞ D17 ⊠ 38–40 Carmine Street/Bedford Street ☎ 212/989-9330 ⊙ Closed Sun
⊚ 1 Houston Street; A, C, E, B, D, F, M 4th Street-Washington Square

FATTY CRAB $$

www.fattycrab.com

Malaysia meets Manhattan in this unpretentious place. It's not exclusively seafood—the short ribs rendang is extremely good. It has another branch in the West Village.
➕ B6 ✉ 2170 Broadway, between 76th and 77th ☎ 212/496-2722 🕐 Daily lunch and dinner 🚇 1 Broadway-79th Street

FOUR SEASONS $$$

www.fourseasonsrestaurant.com

The Four Seasons changed the face of New York dining when it opened in 1959. Choose the dark-wood Grill Room or the romantic Pool Room. Sample dishes include Maryland crabmeat cakes in mustard sauce and filet of bison with foie gras and Perigord black truffle.
➕ E10 ✉ 99 E 52nd Street/Park–Lexington avenues ☎ 212/754-9494 🕐 Mon–Fri lunch and dinner, Sat dinner only, closed Sun 🚇 6 51st Street

GOTHAM BAR AND GRILL $$$

www.gothambarandgrill.com

This restaurant epitomizes New York grandeur, with world-class dishes such as wild striped bass with *haricots verts*. The soaring space is beautifully light and airy.
➕ E16 ✉ 12 E 12th Street/5th Avenue ☎ 212/620-4020 🕐 Mon–Fri lunch and dinner, Sat–Sun dinner only 🚇 L, N, R, Q, 4, 5, 6 14th Street-Union Square

GRIMALDI'S $

www.grimaldis.com

With one of the few coal brick-ovens left in the city, Grimaldi's pizza restaurant dates back to 1905 and has attracted many celebrities, including Frank Sinatra. Constant lines are testament to its reputation. No credit cards.

TERMINAL FEEDING

Here are some highlights at the Food Court at Grand Central Terminal:
Brother Jimmy's BBQ for pulled pork sandwiches and other southern delights.
Café Spice for curries.
Junior's is a great diner with peerless cheesecake.
Magnolia Bakery for scrumptious pastries.
Manhattan Chili Company makes a mean bowl o' red from all-natural ingredients.
Mindy's Kosher Delicatessen does knishes and pastrami-on-rye.

➕ H21 ✉ 19 Old Fulton Street, Brooklyn ☎ 718/858-4300 🕐 Daily lunch and dinner 🚇 A, C High Street; 2 3 Clark Street

GROCERY $$$

www.groceryrestaurant.com

This tiny chef-owned restaurant offers changing nouvelle-American menus. Inside is homey, but the lovely tree-shaded garden takes the cake.
✉ 288 Smith Street/Sacket, Brooklyn ☎ 718/596-3335 🕐 Thu–Sat lunch and dinner, Tue–Wed lunch only, closed Sun 🚇 F, G Carroll Street

Sensational sushi

EAT

A deli to die for

HENRY'S END $$

www.henrysend.com

This neighborhood favorite in Brooklyn has high ceilings, brick walls and an open kitchen. The menu features seasonal fish and locally sourced meat and produce, but the highlight is the Wild Game Festival, winter to spring, with such dishes as elk chop, wild boar or ostrich, plus an award-winning wine list.

H22 ⊠ 44 Henry Street, Brooklyn Heights ☎ 718/834-1776 ④ Daily dinner ⊛ A, C High Street; 2, 3 Clark Street

JACKSON HOLE $

www.jacksonholeburgers.com

This small chain of burger places is useful when all you want is a hefty sandwich in a child-friendly, no-frills environment.

E4 ⊠ 1270 Madison Avenue/91st Street ☎ 212/427-2820 ⊛ 4, 5, 6 86th Street

F8 ⊠ 232 E 64th Street/2nd Avenue ☎ 212/371-7187 ④ Daily breakfast, lunch and dinner ⊛ 6 68th Street-Hunter College

JEAN GEORGES $$$

www.jean-georges.com

One of the world's great chefs, Alsace native Jean Georges Vongerichten is known for his refined, full-flavored Asian-accented cooking. The glass-walled minimalist rooms feel serene and special—perhaps because they were Feng-Shui-ed? Don't miss the molten-center chocolate cake.

C9 ⊠ 1 Central Park West ☎ 212/299-3900 ④ Mon–Sat lunch and dinner, closed Sun ⊛ A, C, B, D 1 59th Street-Columbus Circle

JOHN'S $

www.johnspizzerianyc.com

This converted church has one of just a handful of coal brick-ovens left in the city. It's a great spot for pre- or post-theater pizza.

C11 ⊠ 260 W 44th Street ☎ 212/391-7560 ④ Daily lunch and dinner ⊛ 1, 2, 3, 7, N, Q, R Times Square-42nd Street.

NEW YORK RESTAURANT WEEK

The best dining deal in town is no longer a mere seven-day affair. New York Restaurant Week now takes place twice a year, and lasts for up to a month each winter (beginning late January/early February) and summer (beginning late June/early July). Participating restaurants offer three-course lunches and dinners at a set price (at press time it was $24.07 for lunch and $35 for dinner). Drinks, tax and tip are extra. It's a great chance to dine at some of New York's best and hottest restaurants for a fraction of the normal price. The menus are designed to show off their classic dishes and cooking styles. Check out the dates and restaurants at www.nycgo.com, and book ahead—the best tables go fast!

KATZ'S DELI $

www.katzdeli.com

The site of the hilarious climactic scene in *When Harry Met Sally* is the last deli in a once thriving Jewish neighborhood. Opened in 1888, it upholds traditions: nondescript surroundings and knishes and pastrami sandwiches.

➕ G17 ✉ 205 E Houston Street/Ludlow Street ☎ 212/254-2246 ⏲ Daily breakfast, lunch and dinner 🚇 F, M Lower East Side-2nd Avenue

LOEB BOATHOUSE $$

www.thecentralparkboathouse.com

Leave hectic Manhattan behind at this lakeside place in Central Park. The food is contemporary American but the view is the main reason for coming. The cocktail deck gets busy in summer. Reservations are advised.

➕ D7 ✉ Central Park, nearest to E 72nd Street entrance ☎ 212/517-2233 ⏲ Mon–Fri lunch and dinner, Sat–Sun brunch and dinner, lunch only Dec–Mar 🚇 6 68th Street-Hunter College

MARY ANN'S $

www.maryannsmexican.com

Come here for home-made Mexican food, including fresh tortillas and dishes you won't find at your average Tex-Mex, south of the border atmosphere and margaritas by the pint. Cash only.

➕ C15 ✉ 116 8th Avenue/16th Street ☎ 212/633-0877 ⏲ Daily lunch and dinner 🚇 C, E 14th Street; L 8th Avenue

NOBU $$$

www.noburestaurants.com

It is difficult to get a reservation at this Japanese shrine, part owned by Robert de Niro, but you'll be rewarded by the memorable food

and gorgeous setting. Choose the sea urchin tempura or fresh yellowtail sashimi with jalapeno.

➕ D19 ✉ 105 Hudson Street/Franklin Street ☎ 212/219-0500 ⏲ Mon–Fri lunch and dinner, Sat–Sun dinner only 🚇 1 Franklin Street

NORTH SQUARE $$

www.northsquareny.com

Chef Yoel Cruz's inventive cooking focuses on Mediterranean dishes. The atmosphere is relaxed, and dishes such as lobster risotto, coriander-crusted yellowfin tuna and butterscotch banana bread pudding are sublime. The Sunday jazz brunch has featured Norah Jones, who used to wait tables here.

➕ D16 ✉ 103 Waverly Place ☎ 212/254-1200 ⏲ Mon–Fri breakfast, lunch and dinner, Sat–Sun brunch and dinner 🚇 A, C, E, B, D, F, M West 4th Street–Washington Square

OAK ROOM $$–$$$

www.oakroomny.com

With rising star Eric Hara at the helm in the Plaza's famous Oak Room, there are light bites (lobster mini tacos), salads, platters, and superb burgers and steak, and plenty of old-fashioned glamor.

➕ D9 ✉ Plaza Hotel, 10 Central Park South ☎ 212/758-7777 ⏲ Mon–Fri lunch and dinner, Sat dinner only, Sun brunch 🚇 N, R 5th Avenue-59th Street

EAT

OUEST $$–$$$

www.ouestny.com

This place revitalized the Upper West Side dining scene with its red booths and Euro-American comfort dishes of chef Tom Valenti. His lamb shanks are legendary.

🚇 B5 ✉ 2315 Broadway/83rd Street ☎ 212/580-8700 🕐 Daily dinner 🚉 1 86th Street

OYSTER BAR $$

www.oysterbarny.com

Some reports suggest this 1913 vaulted room in Grand Central Terminal may be resting on past glories, but for a thoroughly New York experience it's hard to beat.

🚇 E11 ✉ Grand Central Terminal, lower level ☎ 212/490-6650 🕐 Mon–Sat lunch and dinner, closed Sun 🚉 4, 5, 6, 7 Grand Central-42nd Street

PER SE $$$

www.perseny.com

If you want to know what all the fuss is about, reserve *way* ahead for Thomas Keller's idiosyncratic cuisine, such as terrine of foie gras and veal cheek or smoked river sturgeon with violet artichokes, peas and mint cream. Try to reserve a table by the window for great views.

🚇 C9 ✉ Time Warner Center, 10 Columbus Circle, 4th floor/60th Street ☎ 212/823-9335 🕐 Daily dinner, Fri–Sun lunch 🚉 A, C, B, D, 1 59th Street-Columbus Circle

PETER LUGER $$$

www.peterluger.com

You get steak, hash browns and creamed spinach, and maybe some tomato-and-onion salad to start—and that's all you need. Peter Luger has been serving the city's best beef since 1887. Reserve early. No credit cards.

🚇 Off map to southeast ✉ 178 Broadway/ Driggs Avenue, Brooklyn ☎ 718/387-7400 🕐 Daily lunch and dinner 🚉 J, Z Marcy Avenue

PICHOLINE $$$

www.picholinenyc.com

The inventive Mediterranean cuisine of Terrance Brennan is as good as ever at his first and very elegant New York address.

🚇 C8 ✉ 35 W 64th Street, between Central Park West and Broadway ☎ 212/724-8585 🕐 Daily dinner 🚉 1 66th Street-Lincoln Center

RIVER CAFÉ $$$

www.rivercafe.com

For a special occasion (jackets required, guys) and drop-dead views across the East River to Manhattan, this is a treat, with classic international food ranging from caviar and wild rock lobster to rabbit and dumplings. Expect great service and elegance.

🚇 Off map to southeast ✉ 1 Water Street, Brooklyn ☎ 718/522-5200 🕐 Mon–Sat lunch and dinner, Sun brunch and dinner 🚉 A, C High Street; 2, 3 Clark Street

---

SHERWOOD CAFÉ $

It started out just selling funky French antiques, but the adjunct café grew until it took over entirely. One of the places that kicked the Brooklyn boom into high gear, the place is always packed, for the French bistro food, the wacky interior and garden. ✉ 195 Smith Street/Baltic Street, Brooklyn ☎ 718/596-1609; www.sherwoodcafe.com 🕐 Mon–Thu dinner, Fri lunch and dinner, Sat–Sun brunch and dinner 🚉 F, G Bergen Street

SCHILLERS $–$$

www.schillersny.com

The man who brought faux-France to Manhattan (Balthazar, Pastis) veers toward the Mitteleuropa deli here. It's quite a scene, though off-hours tend to be peaceful.

🔲 G18 ✉ 131 Rivington Street/Norfolk Street ☎ 212/260-4555 🕐 Mon–Fri lunch and dinner, Sat–Sun brunch and dinner 🚇 F, M Delancey Street-2nd Avenue

SERENDIPITY 3 $

www.serendipity3.com

This toy box/candy store makes the original and best "Frozen Hot Chocolate", as well as burgers, soups and grills.

🔲 F9 ✉ 225 E 60th Street/2nd Avenue ☎ 212/838-3531 🕐 Daily lunch and dinner 🚇 4, 5, 6 59th Street

THE SPOTTED PIG $$

www.thespottedpig.com

You may have to wait for a table (you can't reserve) at this Michelin-starred, Anglo-style gastro pub. Order the *gnudi*, a ricotta-spinach gnocchi that chef April Bloomfield has made her own, with brown butter and sage.

🔲 D16 ✉ 314 W 11th Street/Greenwich Avenue ☎ 212/620-0393 🕐 Daily lunch and dinner, Sat–Sun also brunch 🚇 1, C, E 14th Street; 1 Christopher Street

TOLANI WINE RESTAURANT $$

www.tolaninyc.com

Dine from a menu of global comfort food. Dishes like peri peri prawns, goat curry and North African duck in pastry are served on small plates made for sharing.

🔲 B6 ✉ 410 Amsterdam Avenue/79th Street ☎ 212/873-6252 🕐 Mon–Fri lunch and dinner, Sat–Sun brunch and dinner 🚇 1 79th Street

---

TRAVERTINE $$$

www.travertinenyc.com

The impeccable Italian cooking attracts celebrities to this Nolita favorite. Specialties include their garganelli dish of shitake mushrooms, baby Brussels sprouts and brown butter, and spice-rubbed braised pork belly.

🔲 F18 ✉ 19 Kenmare Street ☎ 212/966-1810 🕐 Tue–Sun dinner, closed Mon 🚇 6 Spring Street; J Bowery

UNCLE NICK'S $$

www.unclenicksgreekrestaurant.com

A fun, festive atmosphere and hearty Greek cooking are hallmarks here. The seafood is straight off the dock.

🔲 B10 ✉ 747 9th Avenue/50th Street ☎ 212/245-7992 🕐 Daily lunch and dinner 🚇 C, E 50th Street

VESELKA $

www.veselka.com

Ukrainian and Polish soul food 24 hours a day. The menu ranges from handmade *pierogi* (dumplings) to goulash and blintzes.

🔲 F16 ✉ 144 2nd Avenue/E 9th Street ☎ 212/228-9682 🕐 Daily 24 hours 🚇 6 Astor Place; F, M 2nd Avenue; R 8th Street

EAT

Sleep

Ranging from luxurious and modern upmarket hotels to simple budget hotels, New York has accommodation to suit everyone. In this section establishments are listed alphabetically.

Introduction

There are plenty of hotel rooms but it is hard to find a comfortable room under $150. If money is no object, reserve a room at the Four Seasons.

On a Budget
For less expensive options, check out the inexpensive chains—Red Roof, Super 8 and others. The city also has some B&Bs, less expensive than the average hotel, which are good value for money. Hostels are the least expensive lodging options (▷ panel, below).

Luxury Living
You'll find first-class luxury hotels throughout the city, although many are in Midtown. Nearly every hotel room comes with air-conditioning, private bathroom, cable TV, telephone, coffee-maker and hand hair dryer, but top-class hotel rooms boast luxe fabrics and linens, high-tech electronics and high staff-to-guest ratios.

Prices
Today there is no such thing as a standard rack rate. Prices change with customer demand, so call the hotel and ask about the best available rate and special discounts. Alternatively, go online to such discount services as hotels.com, quikbook.com or hoteldiscounts.com. Note that taxes will be added to your bill, plus $2 occupancy tax on a standard room and 5.8 percent of the bill.

HOSTELS IN NEW YORK

Big Apple Hostel 119 W 45th, tel 212/302-2603.
Chelsea Center 83 E Essex Street, tel 212/260-0961.
Chelsea International Hostel 251 W 20th Street, tel 212/647-0010.
Hostelling International 891 Amsterdam Avenue at W 103rd Street, tel 212/932-2300.
West Side YMCA 5 W 63rd Street, tel 212/875-4100.
Whitehouse 340 Bowery, tel 212/477-5623.

From top: The Plunge Bar and Lounge at Hotel Gansevoort; guest room in The Shoreham; Crosby Street Hotel; clean lines at The Shoreham

Directory

Lower Manhattan

Budget
Cosmopolitan
Mid-Range
Off Soho Suites
Luxury
Crosby Street Hotel
Ritz-Carlton Battery Park

Downtown and Chelsea

Budget
Carlton Arms
Chelsea Lodge
Hotel 17
Mid-Range
Maritime Hotel
Washington Square
Luxury
Hotel Gansevoort
Inn at Irving Place

Midtown

Budget
Ameritania Hotel

Hotel Wolcott
Mid-Range
70 Park Avenue
The Algonquin (▷ panel, 155)
Beekman Tower
The Hudson
Jolly Madison Hotel
Library Hotel (▷ panel, 156)
Millennium Broadway
The Time
Luxury
Four Seasons
Mandarin Oriental
The Plaza
St. Regis
The Shoreham

Upper West Side

Budget
Hotel Belleclaire
Mid-Range
Excelsior
Hotel Beacon

Sleeping A–Z

PRICES	
Prices are approximate and based on a double room for one night.	
$$$	over $400
$$	$201–$400
$	$100–$200

menu, good sound systems and a special yoga channel on the huge flatscreen TV.

🔢 E12 ✉ 70 Park Avenue/38th Street ☎ 212/973-2400 🍴 Silverleaf Tavern 🚇 4, 5, 6, 7, S Grand Central-42nd Street

AMERITANIA HOTEL $

www.ameritaniahotelnewyork.com
If you want to be in the heart of the theater district then the Ameritania provides mid-class accommodation with the added benefit of spacious common areas and lounge bar.

🔢 C10 ✉ 230 W 54th Street ☎ 407/740-6442 🚇 D 55th Street; N, Q, R 57th Street-7th Avenue

70 PARK AVENUE $$

www.70parkave.com
The first foray into New York by boutique hotel pioneers Kimpton, this 205-room Murray Hill place has a quietly contemporary decor, luxurious extras such as touch-screen room service, a pillow

BEEKMAN TOWER $$

www.thebeekmanhotel.com

The art deco tower in far east Midtown has a lot going for it: well-kept rooms and suites, some with kitchens, most larger than the average with somewhat fusty but comfortable furnishings, a fitness center, room service and two restaurants, including the 26th-story Top of the Tower, with great river and city views.

➕ G10 ✉ 3 Mitchell Place/1st Avenue
☎ 212/355-7300 🚇 6 51st Street

CARLTON ARMS $

www.carltonarms.com

Decorated with crazy murals in the lobby and some of the rooms, this is one of New York's wackiest hotels. Amenities here are minimal but there is a communal atmosphere that makes travelers feel at home. As it says on the business card, "this ain't no Holiday Inn." The 54 comfortable rooms offer good-value accommodation.

➕ F14 ✉ 160 E 25th Street/Lexington–3rd avenues ☎ 212/679-0680
🚇 6 23rd Street

CHELSEA LODGE $

www.chelsealodge.com

The 22 guest rooms of this budget hotel in a brownstone building in the heart of Chelsea are clean and simple, but all come with a shower, sink, TV, and air conditioning in summer and heating in winter. Bathrooms are shared, but for the location it's a bargain.

➕ C15 ✉ 318 W 20th Street
☎ 212/243-4499 🚇 A, C, E 23rd Street; 1, 2 23rd Street

COSMOPOLITAN $

www.cosmohotel.com

No frills in any sense of the word exist at this 150-room, seven-story block in Tribeca. But, if you reckon the real estate rule applies to hotels, you'll love it—the location, location, location is prime. The clean, fully functional rooms vary a good deal in size, so if the hotel isn't full and you're not happy with the room you are shown, ask to see another one.

➕ E20 ✉ 95 W Broadway/Chambers Street ☎ 212/566-1900 🚇 A, C Chambers Street

The bar in Crosby Street Hotel, a fashionable choice in SoHo

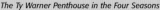

The Ty Warner Penthouse in the Four Seasons

CROSBY STREET HOTEL $$$

www.crosbystreethotel.com

This new kid on the block is from über-cool hoteliers Firmdale. On a cobbled street in the heart of New York's vibrant SoHo, the 86 rooms and suites over 11 floors have full-length warehouse-style windows. The interior design by Kit Hemp is fresh and contemporary, and the hotel has a gym and cinema, a sculpture garden and a selection of one- and two-bedroom suites as well as rooms.

✚ E18 ✉ 79 Crosby Street ☎ 212/226-6400 🚇 4, 6 Spring Street-Lafayette Street

EXCELSIOR $$

www.excelsiorhotelny.com

The location is quite fabulous—steps from Central Park and the American Museum of Natural History, with the subway practically underfoot. The building is grand, too, heavy on the wood paneling, faux-oils and gilt frames. Rooms, though not beautiful in generic brocades and stripes, are fine; even some standard rooms overlook the park.

✚ C6 ✉ 45 W 81st Street/Central Park West ☎ 212/362-9200 🚇 B, C 81st Street-Museum of Natural History

FOUR SEASONS $$$

www.fourseasons.com

The grandiose I. M. Pei building makes a big first impression—all

B&BS

Those who prefer real neighborhoods, authentic experiences and behaving like a local may opt for a B&B. Often these are found in Brooklyn brownstones, where the host has an extra room. Others are empty apartments. The only imperative is to reserve ahead. Another ever-more-popular option is to check the sublet vacation rentals and housing swap listings at www.craigslist.org.

towering lobbies, marble and mezzanine lounges. The rooms don't disappoint. In beiges and creams, they're big, with tons of closets, tubs that fill in no time and, in some, great views. Many consider this Manhattan's top hotel.

✚ E9 ✉ 57 E 57th Street, Park–Madison avenues ☎ 212/758-5700 🍽 The Garden, L'Atelier de Joël Robuchon 🚇 F, Q 57th Street

HOTEL 17 $

www.hotel17ny.com

The kitschy decor almost looks deliberate—its stripey wallpaper, floral bedspread, nylon carpet look seems to hit a chord with rock 'n' roll types and models. That could also be on account of its brownstone New York Gramercy Park location and its dirt cheap rates. It offers shared or private baths.

✚ F15 ✉ 225 E 17th Street/2nd–3rd avenues ☎ 212/475-2845 🚇 L 3rd Avenue

THE ALGONQUIN $$

The Algonquin is forever associated with the only group of literary wits to be named after a piece of furniture: the Algonquin Round Table. The bon viveurs achieved almost as much at the bar here as they did in the pages of the embryo *New Yorker*, with Robert Benchley, Dorothy Parker and Alexander Woolcott well ensconced. The hotel's Rose Room still contains the very table they occupied. ✚ D11 ✉ 59 West 44th Street ☎ 212/840-6800; www.algonquinhotel.com 🚇 B, D, F, M 42nd Street-Bryant Park; 7 5th Avenue

SLEEP

Rooftop pool at Hotel Gansevoort

HOTEL GANSEVOORT $$$

www.hotelgansevoort.com
Fashion-obsessed young creatives consider this illuminated glass tower style-central. The stark guest rooms are furnished in stone and sand colors and equipped with lots of high-tech gadgets. Facilities include a rooftop pool, a spa, the Tanuki Tavern, and the Plunge restaurant and bar.

C16 18 9th Avenue/13th Street 212/206-6700 A, C, E 14th Street; L 8th Avenue

HOTEL WOLCOTT $

www.wolcott.com
Within walking distance of Macy's, the Empire State Building and other attractions, this hotel is great value for money. It has comfortable rooms with private bath and even offers free morning coffee and muffins.

D13 4 W 31st Street, between 5th Avenue and Broadway 212/268-2900 B, D, F, M, N, Q, R 34th Street-Herald Square

THE HUDSON $$

www.hudsonhotel.com
This place is all subdued lighting, trendy staff and minimalist chic and it's a short hop from Central Park (anyone for an early morning run?) and a subway stop with great connections. The Hudson comes alive at night with a fashionable bar and there is a reasonably

HOTEL BEACON $$

www.beaconhotel.com
In the middle of Broadway, on the Upper West Side, the Beacon feels more like an apartment building than a hotel. Some of the 200-plus rooms have kitchenettes.

B7 2130 Broadway/75th Street 212/787-1100 1, 2, 3 72nd Street

HOTEL BELLECLAIRE $

www.hotelbelleclaire.com
Mark Twain lived here, as did Maxim Gorky. Now the early-20th-century building offers 200 clean, minimal guest rooms, with pine furniture and pale apricot-color walls though only the shared-bathroom rooms are budget rate.

B6 250 W 77th Street/Broadway–11th Avenue 212/362-7700 1 79th Street

THE LIBRARY HOTEL $$

Each floor of the hotel is dedicated to a subject category from the Dewey Decimal system and each room has a collection of art and books related to a subcategory. The interior is modern and minimalist. Amenities include multiline phones with high-speed internet access. E11 299 Madison Avenue/41st Street 212/983-4500; www.libraryhotel.com S, 4, 5 6 7 Grand Central-42nd Street

SLEEP

equipped basement gym. Request a room (these are tiny, even by NY standards) overlooking the atrium as they tend to be quieter.

➕ B9 ✉ 356 W 58th Street
☎ 212/554-6000 🚇 1, A, C, B, D 59th Street-Columbus Circle

INN AT IRVING PLACE $$$

www.innatirving.com

With just 12 guest rooms and junior suites, this discreet hotel is set in two 1830s townhouses near Gramercy Park, with elegant decor, period furniture, open fireplaces and a romantic atmosphere.

➕ E15 ✉ 56 Irving Place ☎ 212/533-4600 🚇 4, 5, 6, L, N, Q, R 14th Street-Union Square

JOLLY MADISON HOTEL $$

www.jollymadison.com

This is a very charming Italian-run boutique hotel located on Madison Avenue. It has warmth, elegance and style, but what sets it apart is a blend of 1920s American architecture and modern facilities coupled with extremely comfortable and spacious rooms.

➕ E12 ✉ Madison Avenue at 38th Street
☎ 212/802-0600 🚇 B, D, F, M 42nd Street-Bryant Square

MANDARIN ORIENTAL $$$

www.mandarinoriental.com

This chain is known for its clean lines, its fabulous spas and excellent service. The best of the 248 rooms and suites have lovely panoramic views across Central Park or over the Hudson.

➕ C9 ✉ 80 Columbus Circle/60th Street
☎ 212/805-8800 🍴 Asiate 🚇 A, C, B, D, 1 59th Street-Columbus Circle

MARITIME HOTEL $$

www.themaritimehotel.com

Heat-seeking trendsters will love this quirky 120-room place in the thick of the Meatpacking District. Porthole windows facing the Hudson and navy-blue soft furnishings add to the ship-like feel of the small rooms. It also has a fitness center, a happening bar scene and an Italian restaurant.

➕ C15 ✉ 363 W 16th Street/9th Avenue
☎ 212/242-4300 🍴 Matsuri 🚇 A, C, E 14th Street

View over Manhattan from the Rockefeller Center

MILLENNIUM BROADWAY $$

www.millenniumhotels.com

The Millennium is a good choice for theater-lovers as it's walking distance from 22 Broadway shows and several off-Broadway theaters, as well as Times Square. The high-ceilinged lobby leads to a 52-story building, with 750 guest rooms and suites that have floor-to-ceiling windows for great New York views.

D11 ✉ 145 W 44th Street ☎ 212/768-4400 ⊕ 1, 2, 3, 7 42nd Street-Times Square

OFF SOHO SUITES $$

www.offsoho.com

Since this place opened just a few years ago, its very off-SoHo location on the Lower East Side bordering Nolita has become all the rage. The suites are mini-studio apartments with no decorative advantages whatsoever but with full kitchens, private phones and satellite TV. The "Economy" suites share kitchen and bathroom.

F18 ✉ 11 Rivington Street/Bowery ☎ 212/979-9815 ⊕ F Lower East Side-2nd Avenue; J, Z Bowery

THE PLAZA $$$

www.fairmont.com

With 180 guest rooms and 102 luxury suites, overlooking either Fifth Avenue or Central Park, the Plaza is one of the most expensive hotels in the city. It was also the first hotel in the world to offer in-room iPads—how cool is that?

D9 ✉ 5th Avenue at Central Park South ☎ 212/759-3000 ⊕ N, Q, R 5th Avenue-59th Street

RITZ-CARLTON BATTERY PARK $$$

www.ritzcarlton.com

This glass-sided tower has one thing no other hotel has: the harbor. Decor is pale and contemporary, and the service and facilities are exemplary.

D23 ✉ 2 West Street/Battery Place ☎ 212/344-0800 ⊕ 1 South Ferry

ST. REGIS $$$

www.stregis.com

St. Regis offers Louis XV style in the middle of Midtown. The service is discreet, and the 229 rooms and suites are extremely plush.

St. Regis, a luxurious option in Midtown

➕ E9–E10   ✉ 2 E 55th Street/5th Avenue   ☎ 212/753-4500   Ⓜ E, M 5th Avenue-53rd Street

THE SHOREHAM $$$

www.shorehamhotel.com

The sleek Shoreham Hotel, behind the Museum of Modern Art, has 177 small but nice rooms and suites, with suede walls, diffused lighting and puffy white comforters on the beds. The choice rooms are at the back of the hotel. Extras such as Aveda products, free round-the-clock cappuccino and espresso and a hotel-curated art gallery, plus high-end technology (Bose Wave, plasma screens, XBox 360s) in the better rooms add good value.

➕ D10   ✉ 33 W 55th Street/5th–6th avenues   ☎ 212/247-6700   Ⓜ B, Q 57th Street

THE TIME $$

www.thetimeny.com

Just off Times Square, the 164 rooms and 28 suites sport bold, primary colors. Choose a red, yellow or blue room and you'll find that color not only covering the bed and selected wall parts but also appearing in candy and scent form. A Bose radio and Molton Brown toiletries add value but can't make the small rooms grow any larger, though you can spread out a bit in the small gym and rather swank lounge and restaurant.

➕ C11   ✉ 224 W 49th Street/8th Avenue   ☎ 212/246-5252   Ⓜ N, Q, R, S, 1, 2, 3, 7 Times Square-42nd Street

WASHINGTON SQUARE $$

www.washingtonsquarehotel.com

The only hotel in the heart of Greenwich Village has long been a favorite of musicians, writers and artists. The smart, comfortable rooms have retro-style furniture, while the beautiful lobby has a bright 1930s-style Parisian air and a friendly, multilingual staff. Extras include complimentary breakfast, WiFi and gym; and there are two bars and the North Square restaurant (▷ 147).

➕ E16   ✉ 103 Waverley Place/MacDougal Street   ☎ 212/777-9515   🍴 North Square restaurant   Ⓜ A, C, E, B, D, F, M 4th Street-Washington Square

The Shoreham's bar

SLEEP

106 TRACKS 105

Need to Know

This section takes you through all the practical aspects of your trip to make it run more smoothly and to give you confidence before you go and while you are there.

Planning Ahead

WHEN TO GO

Fall is generally thought the best time to visit New York. In August many New Yorkers are driven out of town by the searing heat. However, during this time lines are shorter, restaurant reservations optional and outdoor festivals at their peak. The city has occasional blizzards in winter, but these rarely cause disruption.

TIME

New York is on Eastern Standard Time, three hours ahead of Los Angeles and five hours behind the UK.

TEMPERATURE

JAN	FEB	MAR	APR	MAY	JUN	JUL	AUG	SEP	OCT	NOV	DEC
39°F	41°F	46°F	61°F	70°F	81°F	84°F	82°F	77°F	66°F	54°F	39°F
4°C	5°C	8°C	16°C	21°C	27°C	29°C	28°C	25°C	19°C	12°C	4°C

Spring (March to May) is unpredictable—even in April snow showers can alternate with shirtsleeves weather—but the worst of winter is over by mid-March.

Summer (June to August) can be extremely hot and humid, especially July and August, when the heat can make sightseeing exhausting.

Fall (September to November) sees warm temperatures persisting into October.

Winter (December to February) can be severe, with heavy snow, biting winds and sub-freezing temperatures.

WHAT'S ON

January/February *Chinese New Year* (Chinatown). *Martin Luther King Day Parade* (3rd Mon in Jan, 5th Avenue, 61st–86th streets).

March 17 *St. Patrick's Day Parade* (5th Avenue, 44th–86th streets).

March/April *Easter Parade* (5th Avenue, 44th–57th streets).

April–October *Baseball*

May *9th Avenue International Food Festival* (9th Avenue, 37th–57th streets ☎ 212/581-7217).

June *Metropolitan Opera park concerts* (☎ 212/362-6000). *Lesbian and Gay Pride Parade* (52nd Street and 5th Avenue to Christopher and Greenwich streets).

June–September *Shakespeare in the Park* (Delacorte Theater ☎ 212/539-8750). *NY Philharmonic park concerts.*

July 4 *Independence Day*

July–August *Harlem Week* (☎ 212/862-8477). *Lincoln Center Out-of-Doors Festival* (☎ 212/875-5000).

August–September *US Open Tennis Championships* (☎ 718/760-6200).

September *Feast of San Gennaro* (Little Italy).

September–October *New York Film Festival* (Lincoln Center ☎ 212/875-5601).

October *Columbus Day Parade* (5th Avenue, 44th–79th streets).

November *NYC Marathon* (Staten Island to Central Park; www.nycmarathon. org). *Macy's Thanksgiving Day Parade* (✉ Central Park West, 77th Street ☎ 212/494-4495).

December *Tree Lighting Ceremony* (✉ Rockefeller Center ☎ 212/332-6868). *New Year's Eve celebrations* (✉ Times Square).

NEW YORK ONLINE

www.nycgo.com
The official tourism website, linked to the NYC Information Center in Midtown, includes a calendar of events, accommodations information, news updates and lots more. The helpful trip-planning section includes themed itineraries.

www.ilovenytheater.com
Offers up-to-the-minute details on show times and tickets, as well as reviews.

http://newyork.citysearch.com
City Search has links to and listings for attractions, entertainment, restaurants, shopping, hotels and more. It also has news, reviews and a directory offering NYC information.

www.nyc.gov
As the official homepage of the City of New York, the site offers links to the Office of the Mayor as well as information about community services, legal policies, city agencies, news and weather and visitor information.

www.ny.com
The "How, Wow and Now" sections let you know what's up on New York's entertainment, dining and nightlife scene. The sports section lists professional events.

www.nymag.com
One of the most comprehensive websites covering what's on in the city, including good restaurant reviews.

www.nytimes.com
Here you'll get an inside look at one of the world's most respected newspapers. The site has links to sections covering everything from world affairs to sports and local gossip.

www.timessquare.com
All about Times Square and the area around, Broadway and its theaters in particular, with booking information.

PRIME TRAVEL SITES

www.fodors.com
A complete travel-planning site. You can research prices and weather; book air tickets, cars and rooms; pose questions to fellow travelers and find links to other sites.

www.iloveny.com
Official NY State site. Information about touring the city and beyond.

www.mta.info
The Metropolitan Transportation Authority updates you on service changes and disruptions, and answers questions about buses and the subway.

INTERNET ACCESS

Anywwwhere Internet
Services have internet cafés located in cafés and restaurants across the city. For locations check www.anywwwhere.com

Kinko's
Have locations throughout the city, many open 24 hours.

Wireless internet is available at many places, including coffee shops, parks, libraries and some hotels.

Getting There

ARRIVING BY LAND

● Greyhound buses from across the US and Canada and commuter buses from New Jersey arrive at the Port Authority Terminal (✉ 625 8th Avenue ☎ 212/564-8484; www.greyhound.com).

● Commuter trains use Grand Central Terminal (✉ E 42nd Street/Park Avenue ☎ 212/532-4900).

● Long-distance trains arrive at Pennsylvania Station (✉ 31st Street/8th Avenue).

CUSTOMS

● Non-US citizens may import duty-free: 1 liter of alcohol (this is the total allowance for wine and/or spirits), 200 cigarettes or 50 cigars and $100 of gifts. (No one under 21 can import alcohol.)

● Among restricted items for import are meat, fruit, plants, seeds and certain prescription medicines without a prescription or written statement from your doctor.

SECURITY

● Always allow plenty of time for clearing security when arriving in or departing from the US.

AIRPORTS

New York has three airports—John F. Kennedy (J.F.K.) (✉ Queens, 15 miles/24km east of Manhattan ☎ 718/244-4444), Newark (✉ New Jersey, 16 miles/25km west ☎ 973/961-6000) and LaGuardia (✉ Queens, 8 miles/13km east ☎ 718/533-3400). Most international flights arrive at J.F.K. For details, visit www.panynj.gov.

LaGuardia Airport
8 miles (13km) to city center. Bus/minibus 40–45 minutes, $12.75

J.F.K. International Airport
15 miles (24km) to city center. Bus/minibus 1 hour, $15.75

Newark Liberty International Airport
16 miles (25km) to city center. Bus/minibus 40 minutes, $16–$20

24km (15 miles) · 16km (10 miles) · 8km (5 miles) · Manhattan

ENTRY REQUIREMENTS

Visitors to New York from outside the US must have a full passport valid for the length of their stay and a return ticket. Under the Visa Waiver Program (VWP), visitors from most European countries, Australia, New Zealand, Japan and others do not need a visa to enter the US for stays of up to 90 days. For a full, current list of these countries check the US State Department website www.travel.state.gov, under "Visas."

All VWP visitors must have machine-readable passports, and all passports issued or renewed after October 26, 2005 must be e-passports containing additional biometric information. Children and infants must each have their own passport; they cannot be included on a parent's passport.

All visitors are required to obtain an electronic authorization to travel at least 72 hours prior to departure. Registration must be done under the Electronic System for Travel Authorization (ESTA™), part of the US Department of Homeland Security. (Visitors who possess a current, valid visa do not need to fill out the ESTA™ application.) Visitors who do not obtain ESTA™ clearance at least 72 hours in advance can be denied boarding or entry to the US. For more information and to fill out the application (in several languages), go to the ESTA™ website: https://esta.cbp.dhs. gov/esta/. Further information is available on: www.cbp.gov/xp/cgov/travel/id_visa/esta/.

There is a $14 fee for the ESTA™ authorization for all visitors in the VWP (▷ panel, right). Payment must be made by credit or debit card when filling out the application online. The authorization is valid for one year from the date of arrival in the US.

FROM J.F.K.
The journey to Manhattan takes around an hour. NYC Airporter express bus (tel 718/777-5111) runs every 20 minutes, 6.15am–11.10pm ($15.75). The SuperShuttle (▷ panel, right) runs to Manhattan 24 hours a day ($23). To reserve, use the courtesy telephone next to the Ground Transportation Desk. A free shuttle bus runs to the A train. Taxis cost $45 plus tolls and tip; use the official taxi stand. The AirTrain to Jamaica (E.J.Z. subway and Long Island Railroad) or Howard Beach (A subway) costs $5 and takes 12 minutes, plus 35–75 minutes to Midtown. It runs every 5–10 minutes, 24 hours a day.

FROM NEWARK
It takes 40 to 60 minutes to Manhattan. AirTrain (tel 888/397-4636) goes direct from all terminals 24 hours a day to Penn Station (A, C, E, 1, 2, 3 subway); follow signs to Monorail/AirTrain. SuperShuttle (▷ panel, right) runs a minibus to Midtown 24 hours a day ($23). A taxi costs $50–$80, plus tolls and a $15 surcharge from Manhattan.

FROM LAGUARDIA
The journey from LaGuardia Airport to Manhattan takes between 40 and 60 minutes. SuperShuttle (▷ panel, right) runs a shared minibus 24 hours (cost $15). Services to Manhattan are also provided by NYC Airporter (cost $12.75; ▷ above). Taxis cost $21–$30 to Manhattan, plus tolls and tip.

ESTA™ ADVISORY
Since the introduction of the ESTA™ requirement and fee, a number of third-party websites have sprung up offering to process the application. These often charge several times the actual ESTA™ fee and are not authorized by the US government. Travelers should be sure to use only the official ESTA™ website, and pay only the $14 fee. A relative or travel agent may submit an ESTA™ application on behalf of a traveler who is unable to do it themselves.

SUPERSHUTTLE
The SuperShuttle is a shared van service that offers efficient and inexpensive door-to-door service from New York's major airports to hotels, businesses and private residences throughout the city. You may have a slightly longer journey time if your stop is at the end of the driver's route, but the set fare can be less than half the cost of a taxi. It is not essential to book in advance; you can simply turn up at the Ground Transportation Desk and wait for the next available shuttle. However, booking in advance online saves time at the airport. You can also book by phone, and ask about any special promotional discounts (such as AAA) that may apply. ☎ 1-800 258-3826; www.supershuttle.com.

Getting Around

● You are unlikely to recover items, but try the following (or call 311, city helpline):

Subway and bus
☎ 212/712-4500

Taxi
☎ 212/639-9675

JFK
☎ 718/244-4225/6

LaGuardia
☎ 718/533-3988

Newark
☎ 973/961-6243

Report a loss quickly if claiming on your insurance.

SUBWAY TIPS

● If your Metrocard doesn't work, don't go to a different turnstile or you'll lose a fare. As the display says, you should "swipe again."
● Check the circular signs on the outside of the cars to make sure you're boarding the correct train. Often two lines share a platform.
● Look at the boards above your head to check whether you're on the up- or downtown side and/or on the local or express track.

TAXIS

NYC–Licenced Taxis
☎ 212/639-9675
www.nyc.gov/taxi

Carmel Car and Limousine
☎ 212/666-6666

Dial 7 Car and Limousine
☎ 212/777-7777

BUSES

● Bus stops are on or near corners, marked by a sign and a yellow painted curb. Any ride costs the same as the subway and you can use a Metrocard or correct change ($2–$25).
● Bus maps are available from token booth clerks in subway stations.
● Buses are safe, clean and excruciatingly slow. The fastest are Limited Stop buses.
● If you pay by Metrocard you may transfer free from bus–subway or bus–bus within two hours of the time you paid the fare.
● A bus map is essential.

SUBWAY

● New York subway lines often close or are diverted for maintenance on weekends, especially in Lower Manhattan. Check the latest information (24 hours) before you travel (tel 718/330-123424; www.mta.info). New York's subway has 24 routes and 468 stations, many open 24 hours (those with a green globe outside are always staffed).
● To ride the subway you need a Metrocard, which you can refill. Swipe the card to enter the turnstile. Refillable Metro cards are more economical than buying single-ride tickets, and you can share the card with a companion. You can top up the card at ticket machines inside the stations for any amount. Unlimited ride Metrocards are also available; with these you must wait 18 minutes between swipes.
● Many stations have separate entrances for up- and downtown services, often on opposite corners of the street. Make sure you take a local train, not a restricted-stop express. Check the subway map and listen to the platform announcements to determine if a train is local or express and will stop at your station.
● Children under 44in (113cm) tall ride free.
● Avoid the less populated subway lines at night. If you do ride at night, stay in the "off hour waiting area" until your train arrives.

TAXIS

● The ubiquitous yellow cab is a New York trademark and, except possibly on very wet or busy evenings, very easy to hail. Hotel concierges can arrange and most bars, restaurants and nightspots will be able to assist. If you want to book something in advance try one of the companies in the Taxis panel (left).

● Cab drivers are notorious for (a) knowing nothing about New York geography, (b) not speaking English, and (c) having an improvisational driving style.

● Tip at least 15 percent. Bills larger than $10 are unpopular for short journeys.

DRIVING

● Driving in New York is not recommended, but a car is essential for going further afield.

● The address of the nearest major car-rental outlet can be found by calling the following toll-free numbers:

Avis, tel 800/331-1212
Budget, tel 800/527-0700
Hertz, tel 800/654-3131
National, tel 877/222-9058

● If driving in New York is unavoidable, make sure you understand the restrictions because penalties for infringements are stringent.

● In many streets parking alternates daily from one side to the other and it is illegal to park within 10ft (3m) either side of a fire hydrant. A car illegally parked will be towed away and the driver heavily fined. Parking is expensive.

● Within the city limits right turns at a red light are prohibited and the speed limit is 30mph (48kph).

● Passing a stopped school bus is illegal and stiff fines can be imposed.

WALKING

New York is one of the few US cities in which the main mode of transportation is walking. Especially if the weather is dry (and if it isn't, umbrella vendors materialize on every other corner), it's far nicer (and often faster) to hike a 10- or 20-block distance than to take the subway, or sit in a cab or bus stalled in traffic. To work it out for yourself, figure one minute per short block (north–south) and two per long block (east–west, on cross streets).

BROOKLYN

If you're visiting sights in Brooklyn, the same subway rules apply (see Subway, left), but you may have to change trains as several local lines operate only in Manhattan (not Queens). The B51 bus runs between City Hall/Park Row in Manhattan and Smith/Fulton streets in Brooklyn on weekdays. It crosses Manhattan Bridge.

VISITORS WITH DISABILITIES

City law requires that all facilities constructed after 1987 provide complete access to people with disabilities. Many owners of older buildings have willingly added disability-access features as well. Two important resources are the Mayor's Office for People with Disabilities (✉ 100 Gold Street, 2nd floor, 10038 ☎ 212/788-2830; www.nyc. gov/mopd) and Hospital Audiences' guide to New York's cultural institutions, *Access for All* (☎ 212/575-7676; www.hospital audiences.org). This online guide describes the accessibility of each place, with information on hearing and visual aids, alternative entrances and the height of telephones and water fountains. H.A. also provides descriptions of theater performances for people with visual impairments.

Essential Facts

- NYC & Company provides free bus and subway maps, calendars of events and discount coupons for Broadway shows ✉ 810 7th Avenue ☎ 212/484-1222; www.nycgo.com ⊙ Mon–Fri 8.30–6, weekends 9–5. There are also information centers at Times Square, the Tavern on the Green in Central Park, Harlem, and kiosks at City Hall and in Chinatown.
- The Visitor Information Center for Times Square is on 7th Avenue between West 46th and West 47th Streets. ☎ 212/869-1890 ⊙ Daily 9–7.

EMERGENCY NUMBERS

- Police, Fire Department, Ambulance ☎ 911
- Crime Victims Hotline ☎ 212/577-7777
- Sex Crimes Report Line ☎ 212/267-7273

ELECTRICITY
- The supply is 100 volts, 60 cycles AC current.
- US appliances use flat two-prong plugs. European appliances require an adapter and a voltage transformer.

ETIQUETTE
- Tipping: waitstaff get 15–20 percent (roughly double the 8.875 percent sales tax); so do cab drivers. Bartenders get about the same (though less than $1 is stingy). Bellhops ($1 per bag), room service waiters (10 percent) and hairdressers (15–20 percent) should also be tipped.
- There are stringent smoking laws in New York. Smoking is banned on public transportation, in cabs, in all places of work, including restaurants and bars, and, since 2011, in all city parks, on beaches and in Times Square.

MAIL AND TELEPHONES
- The main post office (8th Avenue/33rd Street, tel 212/330-3296) is open daily. Branch post offices are listed in *Yellow Pages*.
- Stamps are also available from hotel concierges, online at www.usps.com, at some delis and from vending machines in stores.
- All New York numbers require the area code (212, 718, 646, 347 or 917) when dialing. For long-distance calls, add 1 before the code.
- Hotels often levy hefty surcharges for making calls so it's best to use payphones.
- Watch out for mobile roaming charges that can result in a large bill on your return home; it's best to ask your mobile provider for "bolt-on" packages for use while in New York (especially if you plan to receive emails, use the web or download information).
- To call the US from the UK, dial 001. To call the UK from the US, dial 011 44, then drop the first zero from the area code.

MEDICAL TREATMENT
- It is essential to have adequate insurance.
- In the event of an emergency, the 911 operator will send an ambulance.

- Doctors on Call (24 hours), tel 212/737-1212
- Near Midtown, 24-hour emergency rooms: Roosevelt Hospital, 10th Avenue and 59th Street, tel 212/523-4000
St. Vincent's Hospital, 7th Avenue/12th Street, tel 212/604-7000
- Dental Emergency Service, tel 646/837-7806. An operator will put you in touch with a dentist close to you open 24/7.

MONEY MATTERS
- Credit cards are widely accepted. Visa, MasterCard, American Express, Diner's Card and Discover are the ones that are most commonly used.
- US dollar traveler's checks are often accepted in lieu of cash. It is difficult to exchange foreign currency traveler's checks, even at banks, and fees are high.

NEWSPAPERS AND MAGAZINES
- The local papers are the *New York Times* (with a Sunday edition), the *Daily News* (also with Sunday supplements) and the *New York Post*. The free alternative paper the *Village Voice* includes extensive listings. Also look for the respected *Wall Street Journal* and the pink-hued, gossip-heavy, weekly *New York Observer*.
- As well as the *New Yorker*, *New York* and *Time Out New York*, you may also see the hip *Paper*, the glossy *In New York* and *Where* magazines and the even glossier *Avenue*.

OPENING HOURS
- Banks: Mon–Fri 9–3 or 3.30; some are open longer, and on Saturday.
- Stores: Mon–Sat 10–6; many are open far later, and on Sunday 12–6; those in the Villages, Nolita and SoHo open and close later.
- Museums: hours vary, but Monday is the most common closing day.
- Post offices: Mon–Fri 8 or 9–6. Some open Sat 9–4.
- Opening times given are for general guidance only.

MONEY
The unit of currency is the dollar (= 100 cents). Bills (notes) come in denominations of $1, $2, $5, $10, $20, $50 and $100; coins come in 25¢ (a quarter), 10¢ (a dime), 5¢ (a nickel) and 1¢ (a penny).

TRAVEL INSURANCE
Check your insurance policy and buy a supplementary policy if needed. A minimum of $1 million medical cover is recommended. Choose a policy that also includes trip cancellation, baggage and document loss.

PUBLIC HOLIDAYS
- New Year's Day: January 1
- Martin Luther King, Jr. Day: third Monday of January
- Presidents' Day: third Monday of February
- Memorial Day: last Monday in May
- Independence Day: July 4
- Labor Day: first Monday in September
- Columbus Day: second Monday in October
- Veterans' Day: November 11
- Thanksgiving Day: fourth Thursday of November
- Christmas Day: December 25

CONSULATES

Australia
✉ 150 E 42nd Street
☎ 212/351-6500
Canada
✉ 1251 6th Avenue
☎ 212/596-1628
Denmark
✉ 885 2nd Avenue, 18th Floor
☎ 212/223-4545
France
✉ 934 5th Avenue
☎ 212/606-3600
Germany
✉ 871 UN Plaza
☎ 212/610-9700
Ireland
✉ 345 Park Avenue
☎ 212/319-2555
Italy
✉ 690 Park Avenue
☎ 212/737-9100
Netherlands
✉ 1 Rockefeller Plaza
☎ 877/388-2443
Norway
✉ 825 3rd Avenue
☎ 212/421-7333
UK
✉ 845 3rd Avenue
☎ 212/745-0200

TOILETS

● Almost every department store has facilities, as do many smaller stores and key visitor attractions. Hotel lobbies, bars and restaurants offer rest rooms. Exercise caution when using facilities at public transportation hubs or in less salubrious neighborhoods.

RADIO AND TELEVISION

● NY1 is the main channel serving the New York boroughs and will give you access to news, weather and travel as well as its own take on daily life in the Big Apple.
● WNYC (New York Public Radio) on 93.9 FM and 820 AM is also a good bet for news, culture and music.
● Tickets for *The Late Show with David Letterman* are available at www.cbs.com/late_night/late_show/tickets

SENSIBLE PRECAUTIONS

● Maintain awareness of your surroundings and of other people, and try to look as though you know your way around.
● Avoid the quieter subway lines at night and also certain areas of Brooklyn. Areas of Manhattan once considered unsafe (Alphabet City east of Avenue C, the far west of Midtown, north of about 110th Street and Central Park) are less edgy than they used to be. Still, keep your wits about you in deserted areas.
● Conceal your wallet; keep the fastener of your bag on the inside; and don't flash large amounts of cash or jewelry.

STUDENTS

● An International Student Identity Card (ISIC) is good for reduced admission at many museums, theaters and other attractions.
● Carry the ISIC or some other photo ID card to prove you're a fulltime student or over 21.
● Under-25s will find it expensive to rent a car.

VISITOR PASSES

Two visitor passes offer big savings if you're planning to take in multiple attractions: New York CityPass ($79 adults, $59 children; www.citypass.com) is valid for nine days and covers six top attractions, including the Statue of Liberty, Empire State Building and major museums. If you opt for the Explorer Pass (from $69.99 adults, $47.99 children; www.smartdestinations.com), you can choose 3, 5, 7, or 10 attractions from a list of 45 top sights and tours; valid for 30 days.

Books and Films

BOOKS
Non-fiction
- *The Historical Atlas of New York City* by Eric Homberger (1998), Henry Holt and Company.
- *New York City (A Short History)* by George J. Lankevich (2002), New York University Press.
- *New York: Songs of the City* by Nancy Groce (1999), Watson-Guptill Publications.
- *The New York Times' Book of New York* (2009), Black Dog & Leventhal Publishers.
- *The Gangs of New York* by Herbert Asbury (2008), Dorset Press.

MOVIES
42nd Street (1933), Hal Wallis
King Kong (1933), Merian C. Cooper
Guys and Dolls (1955), Samuel Goldwyn
Breakfast at Tiffany's (1961), Blake Edwards
West Side Story (1961), Robert Wise
Mean Streets (1973), Martin Scorsese
Taxi Driver (1976), Martin Scorsese
New York, New York (1977), Martin Scorsese
Saturday Night Fever (1977), John Badham
Manhattan (1979), Woody Allen
Broadway Danny Rose (1984), Woody Allen
The Cotton Club (1984), Francis Ford Coppola
Desperately Seeking Susan (1985), Susan Seidelman
Radio Days (1987), Woody Allen
When Harry Met Sally (1989), Rob Reiner
A Bronx Tale (1993), Robert De Niro
Pollock (2000), Ed Harris
Requiem for a Dream (2000), Darren Aronofsky
Gangs of New York (2002), Martin Scorsese
The Devil Wears Prada (2006), David Franke
Night at the Museum (2006), Shawn Levy
Sex and the City: The Movie (2008), Michael Patrick King
Julie and Julia (2009), Nora Ephron
The Taking of Pelham 123 (2009), Tony Scott
Brooklyn's Finest (2010), Antoine Fuqua

FICTION

F. Scott Fitzgerald's *The Beautiful and the Damned* (1922), John Dos Passos's *Manhattan Transfer* (1925), J. D. Salinger's *The Catcher in the Rye* (1951) and Truman Capote's *Breakfast at Tiffany's* (1958) are all classic reads. Also recommended are Tom Wolfe's *Bonfire of the Vanities* (1987), *The New York Trilogy* (1988) by Paul Auster, and *New York: The Novel* (2010) by Edward Rutherfurd.

NEED TO KNOW

Index

The Automobile Association would like to thank the following photographers, companies and picture libraries for their assistance in the preparation of this book.

Abbreviations for the picture credits are as follows – (t) top; (b) bottom; (c) center; (l) left; (r) right; (AA) AA World Travel Library.

2(I)–3(II) AA/J Tims; **3(III)** Gansevoort Meatpacking NYC; **3(IV)** AA/J Tims; **4** AA/D Pollack; **5** AA/J Tims; **6t** ©Nick Wood/Alamy; **6b–6/7c** AA/J Tims; **6/7b** Photolibrary; **7t** Photolibrary; **7b** AA/J Tims; **8t** AA/C Sawyer; **8b** ©Pablo Valentini/Alamy; **8/9t** Café Boulud NYC by B. Milne; **8/9b–9t** AA/J Tims; **9tc** AA/C Sawyer; **9bc** © NYC images/Alamy; **9b** AA/J Tims; **10l** AA; **10r** Mary Evans/Classic Stock/H. Armstrong Roberts; **11l** Mary Evans Picture Library; **11r** Courtesy the Lower East Side Tenement Museum, photography by Keiko Niwa; **12–16** AA/J Tims; **16/7t** © Michael Matthews/Alamy; **16/7b–21t** AA/J Tims; **21bl** AA/C Sawyer; **21br–23** AA/J Tims; **24l** photo courtesy of Cooper-Hewitt, National Design Museum Yinka Shonibare MBE (b.1962) England, 2005. Lent by the artist, Stephen Friedman Gallery, London and James Cohan Gallery, New York; **24r** photo courtesy of Cooper-Hewitt, National Design Museum, photo: Matt Flynn; **24/5** photo courtesy of Cooper-Hewitt, National Design Museum; **25l** photo courtesy of Smithsonian Institution Libraries, Cooper-Hewitt, National Design Museum, photo: Matt Flynn; **25r** photo courtesy of Cooper-Hewitt, National Design Museum, photo: Andrew Garn; **26** © Tetra Images/Alamy; **26/7t** AA/C Sawyer; **26/7b** AA/S McBride; **27t** Courtesy of The Ukrainian Museum; **27b** AA/C Sawyer; **28l–32t** AA/J Tims; **32b** © Patrick Batchelder/Alamy; **32/3–33** AA/J Tims; **34/5** The Frick Collection, New York, photo: Michael Bodycomb; **35** The Frick Collection, New York, photo: Galen Lee; **36l–38** AA/J Tims; **38/9** © Philip Scalia/Alamy; **39t–39b** AA/J Tims; **40/1** Christian Kober/Robert Harding; **41l** Édouard Manet *Before the Mirror* (1876), Solomon R. Guggenheim Museum, New York, Thannhauser Collection, Gift, Justin K. Thannhauser; **41r** AA/J Tims; **41b** Vincent van Gogh *Landscape with Snow* (late February 1888), Solomon R. Guggenheim Museum, New York, Thannhauser Collection, Gift, Hilde Thannhauser; **42/3** Mark Bussell, Lincoln Center for the Performing Arts; **43t** Stefan Cohen, Lincoln Center for the Performing Arts; **43bl** Stefan Cohen, Lincoln Center for the Performing Arts; **43br** Mark Bussell, Lincoln Center for the Performing Arts; **44/5** AA/J Tims; **46** AA/J Tims/Chagall®/©ADAGP, Paris and DACS, London 2011/©ADAGP, Paris and DACS, London 2011; **46/7** MoMA/Photo © 2011 Timothy Hursley, Scala, Florence; **48t** AA/J Tims; **48b** © Michal Besser/Alamy; **48/9–54** AA/J Tims; **54/5** © Robert Harding Picture Library Ltd/Alamy; **55t–58b** AA/J Tims; **58/9** © Steven Widoff/Alamy; **59l–61b** AA/J Tims; **62/3** Dempsey and Firpo, Whitney Museum of American Art/Bridgeman; **63** © Richard Levine/Alamy; **64** AA/J Tims; **66l** American Folk Art Museum; **66r** AA/C Sawyer; **67** © AEP/Alamy; **68** Photolibrary; **69l–71l** AA/J Tims; **71r** © Stephen Finn/Alamy; **72** Tetra Images/Getty Images; **73l–74r** AA/J Tims; **75** Photolibrary; **76–79t** AA/J Tims; **79b** © Spencer Grant/Alamy; **82(I)–85t** AA/J Tims; **85b** © Aurora Photos/Alamy; **88t–88b** AA/J Tims; **89** Photolibrary; **90t** AA/J Tims; **90b** AA/S McBride; **91t–97t** AA/J Tims; **97b** Photodisc; **100(I)** AA/J Tims; **100(II)** AA/C Sawyer; **100(III)** The Frick Collection, New York, The West Gallery, photo: Michael Bodycomb; **100(IV)–100(VI)** AA/J Tims; **102t** American Folk Art Museum; **102b** AA/J Tims; **103t** © Matthiola/Alamy; **103c** AA/J Tims; **103b** Mark Bussell, Lincoln Center for the Performing Arts; **106t–106b** AA/J Tims; **107** AA/S McBride; **108t** © Prisma Bildagentur AG/Alamy; **108b** AA/J Tims; **109t** ©Maurice Savage/Alamy; **109b–116/7b** AA/J Tims; **117t** © Patti McConville/Alamy; **117c** AA/J Tims; **117b** AA/C Sawyer; **119–123** AA/J Tims; **124** © Yadid Levy/Alamy; **126** AA/J Tims; **128** © Prisma Bildagentur AG/Alamy; **128/9t** © Jon Arnold Images Ltd/Alamy; **128/9tc** AA/J Tims; **128/9bc** Iwan Baan, Lincoln Center for the Performing Arts; **128/9b–132** AA/J Tims; **136** AA/P Kenward; **138–140t** AA/J Tims; **140tc** AA/C Sawyer; **140bc** Café Boulud NYC by B. Milne; **140b–143** AA/J Tims; **145** AA/J Love; **146** © Kathy deWitt/Alamy; **150** Gansevoort Meatpacking NYC; **152t** Gansevoort Meatpacking NYC; **152tc** Shoreham hotel; **152bc** CROSBY STREET HOTEL www.crosbystreethotel.com; **152b** Shoreham hotel; **154l** CROSBY STREET HOTEL www.crosbystreethotel.com; **154r** Saylor, Durston, Four Seasons Hotels and Resorts; **156** Gansevoort Meatpacking NYC; **157** AA/J Tims; **158** AA/C Sawyer; **159** Shoreham hotel; **160** AA/J Tims.

Every effort has been made to trace the copyright holders, and we apologize in advance for any unintentional omissions or errors. We would be pleased to apply any corrections in a following edition of this publication.

New York City's 25 Best

WRITTEN BY Kate Sekules
ADDITIONAL WRITING BY Donna Dailey
SERIES EDITOR Marie-Claire Jefferies
REVIEWING EDITOR Linda Schmidt
PROJECT EDITOR Dorothy Stannard
COVER DESIGN Guido Caroti
DESIGN WORK Lesley Mitchell
INDEXER Marie Lorimer
PICTURE RESEARCHER Elisabeth Stacey
IMAGE RETOUCHING AND REPRO Sarah Montgomery

ISBN 978-0-307-92811-5

TENTH EDITION

IMPORTANT TIP
Time inevitably brings changes, so always confirm prices, travel facts, and other perishable information when it matters. Although Fodor's cannot accept responsibility for errors, you can use this guide in the confidence that we have taken every care to ensure its accuracy.

SPECIAL SALES
This book is available for special discounts for bulk purchases for sales promotions or premiums. Special editions, including personalized covers, excerpts of existing books, and corporate imprints, can be created in large quantities for special needs. For more information, write to Special Markets/Premium Sales, 1745 Broadway, 3-2, New York, NY 10019 or email specialmarkets@randomhouse.com.

Color separation by AA Digital Department
Printed and bound by Leo Paper Products, China

10 9 8 7 6 5 4 3 2 1

Cover image: gary718/Shutterstock

A04634
Maps in this title produced from map data © Tele Atlas N.V. 2010   Tele Atlas
Transport map © Communicarta Ltd, UK

Titles in the Series